A Way with Words
Vocabulary development activities for learners of English

Book 3

TEACHER'S BOOK

Stuart Redman
and Robert Ellis

Advisory editor: Michael McCarthy

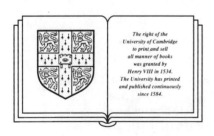

The right of the
University of Cambridge
to print and sell
all manner of books
was granted by
Henry VIII in 1534.
The University has printed
and published continuously
since 1584.

Cambridge University Press
Cambridge
New York   Port Chester
Melbourne   Sydney

Published by the Press Syndicate of the University of Cambridge
The Pitt Building, Trumpington Street, Cambridge CB2 1RP
40 West 20th Street, New York, NY 10011–4211, USA
10 Stamford Road, Oakleigh, Victoria 3166, Australia

© Cambridge University Press 1991

First published 1991

Printed in Great Britain
at the University Press, Cambridge

ISBN 0 521 35922 8   Teacher's Book
ISBN 0 521 35921 X   Student's Book
ISBN 0 521 35028 X   Cassette

GO

Contents

Acknowledgements

Ruth Gairns has been a rich source of ideas and inspiration throughout the last three years and given us enormous support.

In many respects, Jeanne McCarten and Michael McCarthy have been the backbone to this project. Without their wit, wisdom and endeavour, it would not have been possible.

Chitose Sato and Petrina Cliff, for giving permission to use their source material.

The many schools and colleges throughout the world who were kind enough to pilot the material and provide such invaluable feedback.

And finally, thanks to Lindsay White and the rest of the production team at CUP.

The author and publishers are grateful to the following publishers who have given permission for the use of copyright material identified in the text.

HarperCollins Publishers for the extract from *Collins COBUILD Essential English Dictionary* on pp. 22 (top); Longman Group UK Ltd for the extract from *Longman Dictionary of Contemporary English* on p. 22 (bottom).

Introduction

A Way with Words Book 3 is the final book in the series designed to answer the student's perennial question: 'How can I learn more vocabulary?' In doing this it provides a new approach to vocabulary acquisition – an approach which is different from previous vocabulary books in a whole variety of ways.

How is it different?

○ It recognizes that vocabulary does not just mean single words: compounds, phrases and even, on occasion, whole sentences can be *items* of vocabulary. And it recognizes that items of vocabulary form related sets and do not occur at random within conversations and texts. (3.2, 11.2, 13.2, 19.2, etc. provide examples of this.)

○ It consciously teaches students about ways of learning vocabulary so that they become keenly aware of every opportunity for vocabulary expansion which presents itself. (The exercises in Unit 1 introduce the students to key aspects of learning, and many of the *Self-study activities* reinforce this emphasis.)

○ It encourages creative involvement in the process of learning vocabulary in the classroom. The teacher's role is to see that students take full advantage of dictionaries, context, fellow students, mother-tongue, knowledge of the world and so on. Almost all the exercises in the book encourage this kind of self-reliance.

○ It encourages the same sort of involvement in studying alone: every unit includes a separate section of *Self-study activities* specifically designed for self-access. The teacher is also encouraged to photocopy the *Key* in the Teacher's Book so that many other exercises become accessible to students studying alone or correcting their own work in class.

○ It contains a huge variety of exercise types, many of which are based on recent insights into how vocabulary is acquired. In this way it caters for a whole range of learning styles and keeps students constantly motivated.

○ It contains word-building tables to alert the student to common features governing vocabulary formation.

○ There is an accompanying cassette containing recordings for the listening exercises which present new items of vocabulary. It also provides vital help with the pronunciation of difficult items.

○ Finally, *A Way with Words* is different because it brings vocabulary teaching into the mainstream of English Language Teaching. It applies both tried and tested criteria and new techniques to an aspect of ELT which has for too long been considered something of a mystery.

Who is it for?

Book 3 is for upper-intermediate students, many of whom may be in the
final stages of preparation for the Cambridge First Certificate Examination.
Students at a slightly higher level may also benefit from the opportunity to
learn frequently used words that have somehow slipped through the net at
an earlier stage, and the opportunity to practise using words and phrases
which are familiar to them but not yet a part of their active vocabulary.

A *Way with Words Book 3* is designed to be flexible. It can be used: to
supplement a general English course; for a vocabulary option; for self-access;
or to add variety to a reading or listening class. We even know some teachers
who think they could use it as a coursebook – and some students who agree!

How is it organized?

There are 24 units in four groups of six. In each set of six, three deal with
topics which might typically be included in the main coursebooks at this
level, while two further units are centred upon linguistically oriented
features of vocabulary such as affixation, or specific problems associated
with vocabulary such as verb patterns and word order with adjectives and
adverbs. The units are not graded in any way, so you or your students can
pick out an appropriate topic at any stage. If you want to follow up a
particular topic or feature of vocabulary and recycle some of the new items
which have been introduced, there are four *Revision and expansion* units –
the last unit in each group of six: Units 6, 12, 18 and 24.

What vocabulary does it teach?

Each unit actively introduces about 50 items (about 1,000 in the book as a
whole), though full exploitation of the open-ended exercises will
substantially increase this number. The selection of vocabulary is based on:

1 Published wordlists such as *The Cambridge English Lexicon* by Roland
   Hindmarsh (1980, CUP) and the *General Service List of English Words*
   by Michael West (1953, Longman).
2 English Language coursebooks at this level such as the *Cambridge
   English Course Book 3* by Michael Swan and Catherine Walter (1987,
   CUP); the *Collins COBUILD English Course 3* by Jane and Dave Willis
   (1989, Collins); *Headway Upper-Intermediate* by John & Liz Soars
   (1987, OUP); and the various courses preparing students for the
   Cambridge First Certificate Examination.
3 Our own experience (and that of other teachers) of the needs, interests
   and problems of learners of English at this level.

Of course, the final selection is a subjective one and certain types of exercise
tend to attract less useful items to the high frequency items which are being
introduced. Nevertheless, the final selection represents a vocabulary corpus
which is relevant and appropriate for learners at this level.

What does a unit consist of?

Most units provide four exercises which are split into sections so that classes/students can spend as little as perhaps 20 minutes or as much as three hours on a unit if everything is fully exploited. An exercise will typically begin with a section designed as a first introduction to the items to be learned. But a brief introduction is rarely enough to find out how an item is used, where it is used, what its limitations are, how it behaves in certain situations, what other words are likely to co-occur and so on. And, even more importantly, a brief introduction alone often guarantees that the student will forget the item just as quickly as he or she 'learned' it! It is with this in mind that (in parts b, c and d of exercises) the students are engaged in staged practice activities which may involve one or more of the four skills.

This description of a 'typical' exercise is somewhat misleading. The exercises provide an enormous variety of ways to meet and get to know new vocabulary. There are exercises based on problem-solving, grouping words, situations, pictures, sentence building, ordering, grammar, pronunciation, reading, listening, dialogues, discussion, morphology, opposites, dictionaries, errors, and so on.

How *Book 3* builds on *Book 1* and *Book 2*

Book 2 departed from *Book 1* in mixing topic-based units with linguistically oriented units. *Book 3* continues with this same approach, but with an added emphasis on stylistic variation; students at this level should be gaining a wider vocabulary of idiomatic words and expressions, and with it a knowledge of the appropriateness of vocabulary items within a range of situations. (Unit 22 provides examples of this.)

The *Self-study activities* have also been extended in *Book 3* and the lexical input greatly increased. This reflects a belief that students should be more capable of developing vocabulary on their own at this level, and also permits greater freedom for students in the same class to pursue their different needs and interests.

One fundamental way in which *Book 3* does not differ from *Book 1* and *Book 2* is in the continued emphasis on the development of vocabulary learning skills and strategies. *Book 3* offers an even greater range of activities designed to help learners explore different learning skills and strategies, and to find the ideas and techniques which will best facilitate their own retention, storage and retrieval of new items.

Finally, and most important, we hope you and your students will derive as much fun and enjoyment out of using this book as we have had in writing it.

Further reading

Carter, Ronald and McCarthy, Michael, *Vocabulary and Language Teaching*, Longman, 1988.

Carter, Ronald, *Vocabulary: Applied Linguistics Perspectives*, Allen & Unwin, 1987.

French Allen, Virginia, *Techniques in Learning Vocabulary*, Oxford University Press, 1983.

Gairns, Ruth and Redman, Stuart, *Working with Words*, Cambridge University Press, 1986.

McCarthy, Michael, *Vocabulary*, Oxford University Press, 1990.

Morgan, John and Rinvolucri, Mario, *Vocabulary*, Oxford University Press, 1986.

Wallace, Michael, *Teaching Vocabulary*, Heinemann Educational Books, 1982.

1 Learning: Teacher's notes

——— 1 Keeping vocabulary records ———————

a Most students adopt the same approach to vocabulary records: random lists of words accompanied by a translation or definition in English. Few students I have spoken to adopt this system for any clear reason, and most seem to agree that it is not a system which is particularly helpful or inspiring; yet they continue with it. This is a great pity because the mental process involved in organizing words on a page in an interesting and meaningful way can be a very effective learning process. A well-organized notebook also serves as an excellent resource for reference and revision.

You could introduce this activity with a preliminary discussion on written storage. Find out what your students do and why they do it; then show them the page from the student notebook and put them in pairs or groups to discuss the techniques used. At the same time, they will probably discover a few new words and phrases on the page; as they do, encourage them to use some of the techniques as they transfer these words and phrases to their own notebooks. You could also encourage them to copy out part of the page in their own notebook and then add to it in any way they like.

Elicit the techniques used from the group and list them on the board. You can then discuss the value of these techniques with the group.

As a follow-up, give them the group of words in exercise **2** from the *Self-study activities*, and ask them to organize the words in a more meaningful and memorable way. You could do this in class or give it for homework.

Old habits die hard, and if you seriously want your students to give thought to written storage you will need to monitor their storage and repeat this type of activity with other groups of words.

——— 2 Word grammar ———————

a Students need certain grammatical and stylistic information when they are learning new words and phrases, and it is quicker and easier for everyone if there is an understanding of certain terms used in giving that information, e.g. countable and uncountable noun, phrasal verb, gerund, colloquial, etc.

Begin by going through the eight sentences in the Student Book and explain any words or phrases which are unfamiliar. The students can then work on the activity individually or in pairs, using dictionaries to help them if necessary. When you check the answers you could ask the students for more examples, i.e. of adjectives followed by a preposition, separable phrasal verbs, and so on.

b Tell the students that the mistakes in the letter are all connected with the grammatical and stylistic points highlighted in the first activity. Tell them also that they should use the vocabulary in **2a** when they are explaining the errors in the letter to their partner.

This activity is very useful for Cambridge examination classes, and you could construct similar activities of your own based on a different set of potential errors.

—— 3 Taking risks with vocabulary ——

a Give the students the short text and then ask them if they are able to answer any of the questions that follow. When it becomes evident that the students cannot answer the questions with the information they have been given, you can put them in pairs to answer **3b**. This activity will probably take about fifteen minutes and you will need to move round the class and help students with some of their ideas and constructions. When they have finished move on to **3c**.

At the end of the exercise it is worth emphasizing the value of productive use as a learning process, and that students have everything to gain and nothing to lose by trying to use new vocabulary at every available opportunity. Mistakes will occur but this is simply part of the learning process and not something they should be afraid of.

—— 4 Using dictionaries ——

a Go through the example carefully and then ask the students to complete **4a**. If a student is unable to compare their answer with someone who speaks the same language, it is still interesting to see how a different language translates these different meanings of the same verb.

b Follow the instructions in the Student Book.

c Give an example to show the students what they must do:
A: Do you still work at the bank?
B: No, I left two months ago. I work for an insurance company now.
At the end listen to some examples from the different pairs to check that they are manipulating the different meanings of the verb accurately.

Many students tend to neglect common verbs once they have learned one or two meanings of that verb. This is a great oversight because different meanings of verbs such as *leave* and *keep* will be far more important in most communication than a range of obscure verbs; and students should pay special attention to the verbs in English which do not share the same range of meanings as the nearest equivalent in their own language.

SELF-STUDY ACTIVITIES

1 Read through the rubric with the students in class, and check in future lessons to see if any students are making use of the idea. No single idea will be popular with everyone, but if a handful of students are able to make good use of any idea for written storage and revision, the activity will have been worthwhile.

2 As suggested earlier, this activity should be used directly after exercise **1** from the unit.

3 This provides a follow-up to exercise 4 from the unit. Check the answers in the next lesson.

1 Learning:
Key words and expressions

Nouns

ankle	hepatitis (u)
bandage	injury
bruise	knee
cancer (u)	plaster
chin	purchase
cough	quid
cut	risk
damage (u)	shoulder
desert	symptom
elbow	temperature
fault	waist
flu (u)	witness
guess	wrist
hay fever (u)	

Verbs

admit
avoid
bruise
brush sth. up
cough
cut
hurt
pick sth./sb. up
pull out
react
sneeze

Other words and expressions

drop sb. a line	keen (on)
different meanings of *leave*	keep fit
fond (of)	keep + -ing, e.g. I keep getting backache
good (at sth.)	side road
high temperature	sore throat
involved	Yours faithfully

SELF-STUDY ACTIVITIES
---

aerobics	clumsy	train/practise
agile	game/set/match	(un)fit
amateur/professional	get (a bit of / a lot of) exercise	volleyball
athletic	play (a game)	win/lose/draw
badminton	squash	
basketball	sweat	

© Cambridge University Press 1991

1 **Learning:** Key

1

a translation
pictures
topic related words, e.g. symptoms of flu
phonemic transcriptions
grammatical information, e.g. keep + -ing
opposites, e.g. healthy≠unhealthy
example sentences
groups of words which form a compound with the same word, e.g. ache

---

2

a
1	weather	5	fond
2	purchase	6	pick up
3	tell	7	win
4	avoid	8	quid

b some information (uncountable noun)
good at (preposition following *good*)
brush it up (position of pronoun with a separable phrasal verb)
enjoy studying (gerund after *enjoy*)
very intensive course (adjective must come before the noun)
said **or** told me (direct object after *tell*, but not *say*)
very nice to stay (*a great pleasure* is too formal)
write to me (*drop me a line* is too informal)
omit 'I remain' (unnecessarily formal)

4

b
1	definition 1	4	definition 8
2	definition 5.1	5	definition 3
3	definition 2	6	definition 5.2 (there is a case for 4 also)

SELF-STUDY ACTIVITIES
---

3 Here are some examples:
   1 she caught the bus / she caught a cold / she caught the ball
   2 he missed the bus / he missed his family / he missed the goal
   3 I meant to tell you / what does 'fiver' mean? / he means well
   4 I manage a shop / I managed to finish / it's OK, I'll manage
   5 she lost her pen / she lost five kilos / she lost the game
   6 he broke his leg / he broke the law / he broke his racket

2 Putting things in order:
Teacher's notes

a Go through the examples with the class and then allow them five minutes to put the words in the correct column. There are instances, e.g. *broad*, where it is difficult to distinguish between size and shape; it may be wise to warn the students of this fact before they start. Allow them to use dictionaries.

b Follow the instructions in the Student Book.

c This makes an ideal 'warmer' activity for the beginning of your next lesson and provides useful revision of the vocabulary in **1a**.

2

a You could pre-teach new vocabulary here but we prefer to let the students try and work out the answers for themselves. This approach would not be sensible if most of the vocabulary was new, but we would expect upper-intermediate students to be familiar with a number of items in this exercise; the problem is word order rather than meaning.

b When the students have discussed their answers in pairs you can then clarify problems of meaning and word order.

c While the students complete their sentences, move round the class and monitor their answers. When you are satisfied they are putting the adverbs in the correct place in the sentences, you can put them into groups to compare their answers and discuss their different learning strategies.

3

a Follow the instructions in the Student Book.

b Follow the instructions in the Student Book.

c By this stage the students should be more confident about the position of these words, and so the activity is largely to provide further practice, although it does introduce one or two new items. Before the students start, warn them that the missing words may have to go at the beginning or end of the line (some students don't realize this and try to put *enough* in the middle of line 2).

d You could do this on the board with the whole class to ensure the students have an accurate and consistent record of the use and position of these important words.

e This could be omitted or given as homework. We have done it in class with groups who show interest in the story and want to know how it ends.

—— **4**

a Follow the instructions in the Student Book but warn the students that the word *late* is being used here with a new meaning. Allow the students to use dictionaries to help them, and check their answers when they have finished.

b The students could do this in pairs and then compare their answers with another pair when they have finished. If you want a further practice activity, put the students in small groups and ask them to compile a short quiz using these words in their questions. The first three questions in **4b** are examples of the type of question they could produce. When they have prepared their questions (perhaps five or ten), they can give their quiz to another group to answer.

——| **SELF-STUDY ACTIVITIES** |——

1 Putting words along a scale is a useful way of remembering groups of words which are similar in meaning but differ in degree. Encourage your students to add more words to each scale, e.g. where might *laugh* and *smile* go on the scale for the first question?

2 There are various correct answers here so you may wish to check the answers in a future lesson.

2 Putting things in order:
Key words and expressions

Nouns	Adjectives		Adverbs/adverbials
ancestor	alike	leather	almost without exception
descendant	broad	muscular	as a rule
diet	cashmere	nylon	as well
predecessor	curly	pale	barely
prescription	current	pointed	even
successor	fair	scruffy	hardly ever
	filthy	smart	invariably
	former	solid	once in a while
	forthcoming	square	partly
	huge	suede	regularly
	latest	thrilled	repeatedly
		tiny	still
			to a certain extent
			without doubt

Other words and expressions

ex- (president) / ex- (wife)   quite a (warm day)
giggle   scamper
(greatly) relieved   scribble
-ish e.g. greenish   sigh of relief
my late (husband)   there's a good chance that . . .

SELF-STUDY ACTIVITIES
---

accidentally	for a split second	roar with laughter
bravely	grin	screech to a halt
deliberately	jog	sprint
foolishly	pull up sharply	willingly
for ages	reluctantly	

2 Putting things in order: Key

—— 1 ——————————

a

Opinion	Size	Shape	Colour	Material	+ Noun
smart scruffy filthy	tall short huge tiny	thin square pointed long muscular broad	greenish blond (gold) bright pale fair dark	leather suede cashmere steel nylon gold	

b These are possible answers:

1 thin	7 cashmere	13 pointed
2 blond	8 gold	14 scruffy
3 pale	9 broad	15 leather
4 bright	10 muscular	16 filthy
5 smart	11 dark	
6 thin	12 thinner	

—— 2 ——————————

a * shows alternative position for the underlined word.
   1 She <u>hardly ever</u> eats meat.
   2 I <u>partly</u> agree with you*.
   3 Our receptionists are <u>invariably</u> female.
   4 * She <u>generally</u> does her job very efficiently*.
   5 I've <u>repeatedly</u> told him to keep his keys in a safe place*.
   6 * He <u>occasionally</u> loses his temper*.
   7 I think she'll <u>probably</u> get the job*.
   8 I could <u>barely</u> walk when I came out of hospital.
   9 She'll <u>definitely</u> pass the exam*.
   10 I <u>regularly</u> visit my parents*.

––––– **3** –––––––––––––––––––––––––––––––––

a . . . drew up <u>outside</u> at . . .
  . . . is <u>still</u> asleep . . .
  . . . didn't <u>even</u> look . . .
  . . . took <u>quite</u> a . . .
  . . . she <u>still</u> didn't . . .
  . . . getting <u>enough</u> protein . . .
  She <u>hardly ever</u> eats . . .
  He <u>carelessly</u> scribbled . . . *or* . . . form, <u>carelessly</u> closed . . .
  . . . felt <u>greatly</u> relieved . . .
  . . . he <u>also</u> breathed . . .
  . . . we <u>both</u> smiled.

c . . . I <u>hardly ever</u> had . . .
  <u>enough</u> time to . . .
  . . . playing <u>outside</u> when . . .
  . . . come <u>as well</u>, please?
  . . . they <u>even</u> chose . . .
  . . . was <u>quite</u> a . . .
  . . . were <u>still</u> excited . . .
  . . . game. <u>Almost</u> immediately . . .
  . . . They <u>both</u> scampered . . .
  . . . hadn't <u>even</u> noticed . . .
  . . . old enough <u>yet</u> to understand.

––––– **4** –––––––––––––––––––––––––––––––––

a

Past	*Present*	*Future*
former	current	forthcoming
ex-	latest	next
ancestor		successor
predecessor		descendant
recent		
last		
late		
previous		

b 1 former   present/current
   2 present/current   predecessor
   3 successor
   4 latest   last/previous
   5 ancestors

   6 descendants
   7 late
   8 forthcoming
   9 ex-/former
 10 next

SELF-STUDY ACTIVITIES

1 a) grinning → giggling → roaring with laughter
   b) for a split second → for a while → for ages
   c) satisfied → pleased → thrilled
   d) scribbled → wrote → printed
   e) drew up → pulled up sharply → screeched to a halt
   f) jogged → scampered → sprinted

2 a) The documents were <u>foolishly / deliberately / accidentally</u> thrown away.
      (These adverbs could also come at the end of the sentence with no change in meaning.)
   b) I <u>willingly / reluctantly</u> answered all his questions. (These adverbs could also come at the end of the sentence with no change in meaning.) But:
      I <u>foolishly</u> answered all his questions (= I was foolish to answer);
      I answered his questions <u>foolishly</u> (= my answers were foolish).
   c) She <u>foolishly / bravely</u> tried to save the drowning child. (These adverbs could also come after *tried* with no change in meaning.)
   d) When he <u>foolishly</u> pulled out a knife I <u>reluctantly / willingly</u> got out of his way. (*Foolishly* could come after *knife* with no change in meaning; <u>reluctantly</u> and <u>willingly</u> could come at the end of the sentence with no change in meaning.)
   e) He <u>deliberately / reluctantly / willingly</u> spent the whole day in bed. (These adverbs could come at the end of the sentence with no change in meaning.)

3 Character and personality:
Teacher's notes

1

a Students who understand and enjoy irony often derive great satisfaction from this exercise, learning not only the target items but also many of the quotations as well. Other students find the quotations puzzling and unhelpful, so you should make an assessment of your class before using this exercise. If in doubt, give it as a self-study activity and make it optional.

  If you use it, allow your students ten minutes to do the activity and then put them in pairs to compare and discuss their answers. Clarify any problems at the end.

b If the students spent a lot of time discussing their answers to **a**, this activity may be redundant. If so, omit it.

c If the students cannot think of any quotations, ask them to find one for homework.

2

a Explain the rubric carefully before putting the students into pairs or groups to do the activity. They will probably meet three or four new words and phrases in the sentences, e.g. *I'm not bothered, bound to, make a fuss*; you could pre-teach these items or allow the students to use context and/or dictionaries to find the meaning. If they use dictionaries you must tell them to check the meaning against the context, as *bother* and *bound to* have more than one meaning. Discuss the answers with the class. If there is disagreement, see if the students are able to justify their answers.

b Students will now have built up profiles of the three characters, and it is interesting to see how they interpret these characters: for some students the third character is selfish and ruthless, while for others the character is seen as ambitious and dynamic. The discussion arising out of these differences should help to consolidate meaning, although students may need to use dictionaries initially to look up certain words, e.g. *frank* and *ruthless*. It is also worth discussing with the group the degree to which these words can be used positively and/or negatively. For example, can *ruthless* be used as a positive adjective?

c This activity changes the focus to expressions with *do* and *make* and helps to consolidate a number of examples from the first text. When the students have finished you could have a short brainstorming session to see how many more examples they can list.

d 🔲 As this is a long activity it may be wise to leave the listening component and use it for revision purposes in the next lesson.

3
---

a Begin by asking the students to explain the difference between a translator and an interpreter. The students can then attempt the first activity in pairs, with the help of dictionaries. Discuss the answers with the class and put them on the board (disputed answers can go on the board with a question mark).

b The students read the text and check their answers.

c Students should be familiar with these link words, but they are always worth practising and this text is rich in examples. They can write their own examples comparing journalists and novelists, in pairs or individually.

SELF-STUDY ACTIVITIES
---

1 This word building activity extends vocabulary from exercise **1a**, and also alerts students to the Word-building tables at the back of the book, which they can use as a reference source throughout the course.

2 Make sure the students realize they must think of necessary qualities for a job, not what people actually do in these jobs.

3 This exercise will be of greater interest if your students know each other well.

3 Character and personality:
Key words and expressions

Nouns

acquaintance
bravery
conceit
conscience
cowardice
critic
cynic
initiative
interpreter
optimist
pessimist
translator

Adjectives

academic
accurate
arrogant
articulate
cynical
dynamic
easy-going
flexible
fluent
frank
honest
intuitive
methodical
modest
outgoing
quick-witted
ruthless
selfish
self-confident
thorough
vague

Other words and expressions

bound to . . .
by contrast
do homework
do one's best
do something, e.g. I didn't do anything
 at the weekend.
hide one's feelings
I couldn't do without it
I'm not bothered about . . .
-ish, e.g. youngish
it doesn't do any good -ing . . .

make a fuss
make a good job of (sth.)
make a mistake
make a point of (doing sth.)
make an effort
make an excuse
speak one's mind
whereas
while

SELF-STUDY ACTIVITIES

ambition
arrogance
boredom
brave
conceited
conscientious
coward
cowardly
critical (of)
criticism
cynical
cynicism
dynamism
honesty
laziness
modesty
optimism
optimistic
pessimism
pessimistic
rely (on)
ruthlessness
self-confidence
selfishness
shyness
(un)reliability
weakness

3 **Character and personality:** Key

─── **1** ───────────────────────

a 1 initiative   6 conscience
   2 an optimist   7 an acquaintance
   3 a critic   8 conceit
   4 bravery   9 a bore
   5 a pessimist   10 a cynic

─── **2** ───────────────────────

a First character: sentences 1, 5, 8 and 10.
   Second character: sentences 2, 4, 9 and 11.
   Third character: sentences 3, 6, 7 and 12.

b Possible answers are:
   First character: shy, modest, weak, practical, boring and honest.
   Second character: lazy, vague, easy-going, selfish, unreliable and honest.
   Third character: self-confident, arrogant, dynamic, ambitious, ruthless,
   frank, practical, selfish and honest.

d The tape suggests it is the first character: modest, hard-working,
   practical, etc. Expressions he uses with *do* or *make* are:
   make an effort   made up my mind
   doing things   make a point of (doing sth.)
   makes a big difference (couldn't) do without (sth.)
   makes it so difficult   made quite a good job of (sth.)

b According to the text, the qualities are:

Interpreters
fluent speakers
ability to summarize
flexible
outgoing
good (short-term) memory
intuitive
quick-witted
articulate
youngish

Translators
methodical
academic
thorough
patient
good (long-term) memory

SELF-STUDY ACTIVITIES

1 You should find all the answers in the Word-building tables at the back of the Student Book.

4 **Nouns:** Teacher's notes

1

a Go through the examples carefully and make sure the students understand the difference between countable and uncountable nouns. Point out also that a good dictionary will indicate whether a noun is countable or uncountable:

> **telex** /tɛlɛks/, **telexes, telexing, telexed.** 1 N UNCOUNT
> Telex is an international system of sending written messages immediately from one place to another. You type a message on to a machine, and the machine sends the message by telegraph to another machine, which prints it. EG *We had our own telex facilities.*
> 2 A **telex** is 2.1 a machine that transmits telex N COUNT messages. EG *I asked the telex operator if he could get my stories off first.* 2.2 a message that you send N COUNT or that has been received and printed by telex. EG *He burst in with an urgent telex.*

> **tel·ex**[1] /'telɛks/ *n* **1** [U] the system of sending messages from one TELEPRINTER to another by telephone line, SAT-ELLITE, etc.: *We'll give you our reply by telex.* **2** [C] a message received or sent in this way: *A telex has just arrived from Hong Kong.*

When the students have completed the exercise they can compare their answers before you check them with the class. In particular, highlight the use of:
    Have you got any room . . .?
    Did you have any trouble getting . . .?
Without these constructions students often make mistakes:
    Have you place . . .?
    Did you have troubles to come . . .?

b If your students possess good monolingual dictionaries, this activity could be done for homework.

2

a Go through the examples and add more; e.g. *elephant's trunk*; *Spain's economy*; *the foot of the mountain*. The students can then do the exercise, which you should check before moving on.

b Explain any new words, e.g. *cage*, *shed* and *ladder*, and then give the students about ten minutes to develop a story individually or in pairs. When they have finished they can read their stories to another student or pair, before listening to the tape.

c 🔲 Follow the instructions in the Student Book.

────── **3** ─────────────────────────────────────

a Once again, go through the examples carefully and make sure the students recognize that the adjective becomes singular, i.e. *a ten-minute walk* and not *a ten-minutes walk*.

b The choice of adjective will depend on the noun it is modifying, so the students will have to understand the nouns being used in the sentences, e.g. *jug*, *fence*, and so on. Check the answers when they have finished.

c This exercise has particular value and relevance if your students have just arrived in England or are about to go to England. If that is not the case, you may decide to omit the activity, although we have found that students are fascinated by English weights and measures and they are very motivated to do the exercise.

────── **4** ─────────────────────────────────────

a There are no rules which determine whether a compound is written as one word, two words, or hyphenated; the students will simply have to check in a dictionary if they are not sure, and even then, they may find discrepancies between different dictionaries. You might also take this opportunity to show how two words may combine in a compound and a genitive construction but with a different meaning, e.g. *dogfood* (compound used for food given to dogs in general) and *the dog's food* (the food of a particular dog).

I have found the exercise often works best in pairs. Put two students together to work on **a** while a different pair works on **b**. Mix the pairs for part **c** and then check the answers.

SELF-STUDY ACTIVITIES

1 It is important to check the answers to this exercise as these words are a common source of student error, particularly in First Certificate compositions.

2 The most important thing about an exercise of this type is not what the students are being asked to do, but simply the provision of a task which may motivate the students to pick up a piece of written English and study it in their own time; they will probably learn all sorts of vocabulary quite unrelated to noun constructions.

3 This is more relevant to adult learners. With younger students you may decide to omit it.

4 Nouns:
Key words and expressions

advice (u)
backache
bike
blackboard
black market
blade
bow-tie
box office
branch (of a tree)
cage
cardboard
coat hanger
corkscrew
cruise
delay
envelope
experience (u)

fence
foot
furniture (u)
gallon
headphones
height
inch
information (u)
jug
ladder
lamp-post
luggage (u)
news (u)
paw
pickpocket
pint
pocket money

pound (weight)
reward
roof
room (= space) (u)
ruler
shed
spaghetti (u)
surface
table mat
toothpick
tower
trouble
weather (u)
wine list
writing paper

Other words and expressions

five-star hotel
grab hold of

three-course lunch
two-litre engine

SELF-STUDY ACTIVITIES

assistant manager
deputy manager
dress (u) (c)
equipment (u)
flu (u)
job (c)
luck (u)
personal assistant
personal secretary

personnel manager
political leader
political party
training (u)
vice-chairman
vice-president
work (u) (c)
training (u)
travel (u)

4 Nouns: Key

—— 1 ——

a
1 Have you got much luggage?
2 The spaghetti is ready.
3 The latest news from China is disturbing.
4 She owns a few small companies.
5 You can put the furniture over there.
6 Is there any room left on the bus?
7 I sent the packages this morning.
8 Did you have any trouble getting here?
9 There are lots of disadvantages.
10 You can get the information from reception.
11 I asked the teacher for some advice.
12 How much experience have you got as a journalist?

b The nouns which can be countable are:
— *room*, e.g. We have a spare room in the cottage.
— *experience*, e.g. Living in China was a wonderful experience.
— *luggage, spaghetti, news, furniture, information* and *advice*, can all be used as countable nouns when preceded by *a piece of*, e.g. He gave me a valuable piece of advice.

—— 2 ——

a
the height of the tower
a summary of the facts
the blade of the knife
the back of the envelope
the surface of the water

Beethoven's Fifth Symphony
the cat's paw
Britain's balance of payments
an hour's delay
the government's responsibility
my nephew's bike
Mary's jewellery

——— 3 ———

b Here are some possible answers:
1	five-hour (delay)	6	six-foot (fence)
2	ten-year-old (child)	7	two-litre (jug)
3	five-star (hotel)	8	two-litre (engine)
4	ten-day (cruise)	9	three-course (lunch)
5	three-mile (drive)	10	ten-thousand-pound (reward)

c
1	a two-mile walk	4	a one-gallon can of petrol
2	a two-metre fence	5	a two-pint jug
3	a twelve-inch ruler	6	a ten-pound bag of sand

——— 4 ———

a
writing paper
postbox / post office
backache / backhand
cardboard / blackboard
pocket money
headache / backache
postcard / phone card
headache / headphones
paperback / paper money

money market / black market
toothache / toothpick
money market / money box
black market / blackboard / black box
handwriting
post office / box office / head office
postbox / phone box
pickpocket
cardphone / headphones

b
toothpick	newspaper	street lamp
shoe shop	pepper pot	credit card
tablecloth	bow-tie	picture frame
phone box	lamp-post	hatstand
litter bin	traffic light	table mat
taxi driver	salt cellar	coat hanger
handbag	wine bottle	earring
letter box	police officer	dinner plate

SELF-STUDY ACTIVITIES

1 training (u)   work (c/u), e.g. work is good for you (u)
  luck (u)   a magnificent work of art (c)
  flu (u)   dress (c/u), e.g. dress is important (u)
  travel (u)   she wore a blue dress (c)
  job (c)
  equipment (u)

3 deputy leader   party chairman
  party leader   political party
  vice-president   personal secretary
  political leader   deputy chairman
  personnel manager   assistant manager
  assistant secretary deputy manager
  vice-chairman

5 Changes: Teacher's notes

—— 1 ——

a When the students have underlined the verbs indicating change, put them in pairs to discuss the possibility of substituting one verb for another in different parts of the text. You can then discuss this question with the whole class.

b This multiple-choice test usually uncovers further problems that the students have in distinguishing between these verbs: *adjust* vs. *adapt*, and *adapt* vs. *alter* are particularly difficult, and you should not expect students to be able to resolve all of these difficulties in a single exercise.

c It is interesting to see how different students tackle this problem: some use translation; some write definitions in their first language; some write lots of sentence examples; some produce little diagrams. In general, the exercise is a very good illustration of the value and limitations of translation.

—— 2 ——

a It is important the students do not look at the text, so it may be wise to write the words on the board at this stage.

b When the students have discussed their answers they can read the text and fill in the gaps. If they cannot think of an appropriate word, tell them to write in a suitable word from their own language.

c If students have answers which are totally wrong, you should look at the context and try to find out why they were unable to find a logical answer. This may be time-consuming but guessing words from context is a valuable skill and some students will require individual attention to help them. If this is the case, you could ask the rest of the class to do one of the self-study activities to keep them occupied.

d This can be omitted if you are short of time.

3

---

a Although the majority of students do not use the phrases in the list, the meaning is usually quite clear to them in the context of the activity so no pre-teaching should be necessary. The questions themselves present the learners with a thinly disguised activity to practise transitive and intransitive verbs, e.g. *raise* vs. *rise*. If the students seem unable to manipulate these verbs accurately in the discussion activity, you may have to intervene and highlight this aspect of word grammar before allowing them to continue.

This is also an activity where your own knowledge of the students and the school may suggest further questions which will provoke more discussion than those in the book; in this case, don't hesitate to amend the exercise in order to derive as much student interaction as possible in **3b**.

4

---

a [cassette] Before playing the cassette tell the students to read through the questions to make sure they understand the vocabulary, e.g. *extend, get rid of* and *abolish*. Then play the cassette and put the students in pairs to discuss their answers. If the students found it difficult and cannot agree on their answers, play the cassette again and discuss the answers with the group.

b If the students are all familiar with the town in which they are studying, you could ask them to think of places in the town which would be accurately described by some of the adjectives.

SELF-STUDY ACTIVITIES
---

1 This is an important set of verbs so check the answers in a future lesson.

2 With a monolingual group, you could ask them to think of 'new' words and phrases in their own language; some of them may well be English in origin. Your students may also be interested to know that English does not have a board of academics who decide whether to admit a new word into the language; new words and phrases are adopted in English and entered in dictionaries if they are used by enough people. This is one reason why English is such a dynamic language, constantly changing and evolving.

3 This can be omitted if you detect no great enthusiasm for it. However, it is quite a common essay title in Paper 2 of the First Certificate exam.

5 Changes:
Key words and expressions

Nouns	Verbs	Adjectives
bus fare	abolish	disposable
dishwasher	adapt	essential/crucial
fees	adopt	(il)legal
foundations	alter	obsolete
gum disease	extend	old-fashioned
hygiene	go up / rise	organic
nappy	install	posh
operation	put up / raise	rare
priest	swap	run-down
surgery	switch	shabby
tap	transform	smart
tinned food	vary	trendy
wrist	wipe out	unsafe
		well-equipped

Other words and expressions

be fed up
get rid of
it would affect me (quite a lot)
it wouldn't bother me at all

to the $\begin{cases} \text{north} \\ \text{south} \end{cases}$

SELF-STUDY ACTIVITIES

cure	heal	ageism	passive smoking
decline	increase	catalytic converter	perestroika
dissolve	melt	football hooliganism	satellite broadcasting
expand	reduce	hands-on	the greenhouse effect
fade	shrink	head-hunter	yuppies
grow	swell		

© Cambridge University Press 1991

5 Changes: Key

1

---

a The verbs are:

adapt (line 2)	alter (line 5)	swap (line 8)	transform (line 10)
adjust (line 3)	switch (line 6)	change (line 8)	vary (line 11)

b 1 c   2 a/c   3 c   4 a/b   5 b/c   6 b   7 b/c   8-a/d

2

---

a According to the article all the things in the list will disappear.

b The missing words are listed in the Student Book in exercise **2c**.

4

---

a ⊏▭⊐
1 The pool.
2 A cafeteria.
3 It has been redesigned and replaced by a sauna and sunbeds.
4 The baths because there was a public health problem.
5 The men's and women's changing rooms, because more women go now and they needed the additional space.
6 Multi-gym machines, exercise bikes, weight training equipment, etc.
7 The entrance. They have moved the reception desk to the other side.
8 The members only rule.

b
Old	New
run-down	trendy
shabby	modern
unsafe	smart
old-fashioned	well-equipped
	posh

© Cambridge University Press 1991

SELF-STUDY ACTIVITIES

1a 1 shrink   2 melt   3 dissolve
    4 expand (melt)   5 fade   6 heal

2 *satellite broadcasting*: television which is transmitted from a satellite
   passive smoking: breathing the smoke from other people's cigarettes
   head-hunter: someone who tries to recruit a particularly good person for a
   particular job
   football hooliganism: violence related to people who go to football matches
   the greenhouse effect: the warming effect on the atmosphere when the heat
   cannot escape because of a layer of gases
   yuppies: young people with very well paid jobs usually in financial organisations
   perestroika: reconstruction (from Russian)
   hands-on: practising by using the machine in question, usually a computer
   ageism: treating people as inferior because they are old
   catalytic converter: extracts harmful gases from the exhaust of a car

6 Revision and expansion:
Teacher's notes

—— **1** ——

This revision activity draws together some transitive and intransitive verbs that are commonly confused. At the end of the exercise make sure the students are aware of the difference. You could, for example, ask them why *beat* is the correct answer to question 1 but cannot be the answer to question 2.

—— **2** ——

If you teach a monolingual group, you could ask them for words in their own language which are commonly shortened, and whether foreign learners of their language might be surprised or misled by this.

—— **3** ——

There are a number of correct answers to most of these questions, so when the students have finished tell them to move round the class listing the different correct possibilities.

—— **4** ——

Students usually prefer to work on crosswords individually. Set them a time limit, e.g. ten minutes, and then they can move round the class checking their answers.

—— **5** ——

▭ Follow the instructions in the Student Book. You can use this type of exercise to teach phonetic symbols so that the students will be able to discover the pronunciation of words by themselves using the phonemic transcriptions in their dictionaries. For example:

hay	pale	vary	vague	phrase
/heɪ/	/peɪl/	/veəri/	/veɪg/	/freɪz/

—— **6** ——

If your students are not interested in politics, you could ask them to discuss the different adjectives with reference to a successful teacher.

—— **7** ——

Move round the class and monitor the questions carefully before putting the students into pairs for further practice.

—— **8** ——

You could give this writing activity for homework and ask the students to compare their stories in the next lesson.

—— **9** ——

Follow the instructions in the Student Book. This is the type of activity you can use on a regular basis as a 'warmer' at the beginning of a lesson.

—— **10** ——

This is another opportunity to consolidate your students' understanding of phonetic symbols. If you regularly spend a few minutes on these symbols it is surprising how quickly students can absorb them and make use of them in their own learning. It is a valuable self-study skill.

—— **11** ——

When the students have finished, put them in groups to discuss their answers before checking with the whole class.

—— **12** ——

Storage is a very important aspect of vocabulary learning and it needs to be addressed on a regular basis. We would recommend that you monitor your students' vocabulary records regularly and encourage them to exchange ideas on this important topic. The revision activity in **b** provides one way of revising previous vocabulary items from a different perspective, but your students may have their own methods and techniques which you could discuss with the class and experiment with.

6 Revision and expansion:
New words and expressions

advertisement/advert *or* ad
compact disc
explain (+ wh-) vs. show (trans.), e.g. he explained what to do *or* he showed
 me what to do
laboratory/lab
mathematics/maths
personal computer/PC
sales representative/sales rep
tube
veterinary surgeon/vet

6 Revision and expansion: Key

1

1 beat
2 won
3 gone up/risen/increased
4 raised/put up/increased
5 gone down/fallen
6 reduced/lowered/cut/put down
7 told
8 said
9 explain/describe
10 show/tell

2

flu   gym   vet   sales rep   maths
bike   fridge   lab   ad/advert   PC

3

Possible answers are:
1 The title of the play / book / film.
2 The blade of the knife.
3 A bag of shopping / sweets.
4 Verdi's opera / Aida.
5 Picasso's painting / Guernica.
6 The vet's surgery.
7 A twelve-inch ruler.
8 A ten-pound note / salmon.
9 A branch of the tree / bank / company.
10 A summary of the novel / article.
11 A tube of glue / toothpaste.
12 Beethoven's symphony / sonata.
13 Shakespeare's play / Macbeth.
14 An hour's journey / delay.
15 A six-foot wall.
16 The edge of the roof / cliff / table.

—— 4 ——

—— 5 ——

1 ruin   2 heal   3 bother   4 vary   5 huge

—— 6 ——

This is too subjective to give answers.

—— 7 ——

Possible questions are:
1 Do you go to the cinema a lot?
2 Do you still smoke?
3 Would it worry you if you had to move to a different town?
4 Did she give you something to eat?
5 Did you like her last record?
6 Is he the current leader?
7 Have you got a bandage?
8 Was it badly damaged?
9 What happened to your jumper?
10 Did you have any trouble getting here?

——— 8 ———

This is a possible description of the accident:

I had an accident when I was driving to the shops. A car came out of a side road and we collided. He was trying to come out quickly because there was a car coming in the opposite direction, and he couldn't see me because of the parked cars near the junction. I braked when I saw him but it was too late. Fortunately nobody was hurt, and at least the driver was prepared to admit that it was his fault, and he's going to pay for all the damage.

——— 9 ———

Possible answers are:

conceited ≠ modest
deliberate ≠ accidental
hurt = injure
shy ≠ self-confident
get rid of = throw away
           ≠ keep
successor ≠ predecessor
quid = pound (money)
trendy = fashionable

purchase = buy
foolish = stupid
        ≠ intelligent
huge = enormous
      ≠ tiny
rare = unusual
     ≠ common

reluctant = unwilling
          ≠ willing
fond of = keen on
bravery ≠ cowardice
essential = crucial
fluent ≠ hesitant
extrovert = outgoing
          ≠ introvert
posh = smart
      ≠ scruffy

as a rule = generally
without a doubt = certainly
once in a while = occasionally
to a certain extent = partly
barely = hardly

——— 10 ———

/ ɪ /	/ aɪ /	
symptom	reliable	agile
prejudice	hepatitis	wipe out
wrist	pint	
cynic	shy	
promise	dynamic	
symphony	tiny	

© Cambridge University Press 1991

—— **11** ————————————————————

Here are some possible answers:

1	ice cream	7	a rule
2	sugar	8	clothes
3	denim (jeans)	9	a watch strap
4	metal	10	places
5	morals	11	a building
6	work routine	12	death

7 **Work:** Teacher's notes

1
---

a It is important the students do not see the Stress League during the first activity, so write the five jobs on the board. If the students are unhappy that the jobs are too vaguely defined, make them more specific, e.g. an assistant manager in a bank, a secondary school teacher in a medium-sized town. Put the students in groups and put some of their answers on the board when they have finished.

b When the students read through the list you may need to explain some of the jobs, e.g. vicar, estate agent, solicitor, etc.
You can provide further practice by asking the students to group the jobs in different ways. For example:
— How many of the jobs require manual skills?
— How many of the jobs require a person to be good at figures?
— How many jobs involve risking one's life?

2
---

a When the students are filling in the boxes, move round the class and help them with ideas they are trying to express.

b When the students read the text encourage them to look for better ways of expressing particular ideas. For example, if a student has written 'not enough money' as a cause of stress, tell them to look for ways in which this concept is expressed in the text; in this case it is 'financial insecurity'. You can obviously expand on this theme by asking them to consider stress levels in their own work, or causes of stress in learning a foreign language.

3
---

a Students should be able to deduce most of the answers without the need for pre-teaching. You can clarify any problems when you go through their answers.

b When you explain the examples highlight the rising intonation on 'sorry?' and 'I beg your pardon?' Get the students to practise the dialogues until they can paraphrase each expression without hesitation.

c This further practice activity often creates a need for more vocabulary, e.g. shiftwork, career prospects, etc. If you are familiar with your students' jobs, it may be wise to anticipate some of the questions and pre-teach certain items before they begin.

 4

a Students can do this in pairs or small groups, using dictionaries to look up new words as they work through the list. When they have finished, they can compare their answers with other groups before you establish (or try to establish) a standardized answer with the whole class.

b This can be omitted if you are short of time.

SELF-STUDY ACTIVITIES

1 Students are unlikely to find some of these idiomatic expressions in a small bilingual dictionary, so this exercise may be unrealistic unless they have access to good dictionaries.

2 Check the answers to this exercise in a future lesson.

3 This type of activity can be particularly useful for adult students studying English in their own country as it introduces a learning task into their everyday working lives.

7 Work:
Key words and expressions

Verbs	Nouns	Adjectives
apologize	absenteeism	demanding
attend	apathy	freelance
cancel	blood pressure	hostile
complain	fringe benefits	responsible (for)
compromise	heart disease	rewarding
delegate	industrial relations	satisfying
fire	mental illness	skilled
involve	overtime	
mark (homework)	perks	
obey	recruitment	
resign	stress	
sack	training	
sign	turnover	
take sb. on		

Other words and expressions

go on strike
hand in one's notice
heavy drinking
I beg your pardon
in a (good / bad) mood
in charge of
on the outskirts of

set a good example
take risks
tell lies
under scrutiny

Jobs and professions

estate agent
librarian
miner
politician
stockbroker
vet
vicar

SELF-STUDY ACTIVITIES
---

golden handshake
high-flier
pull my/one's socks up
real slave driver
up to my eyes . . .
workaholic

backlog
breakdown
downfall
output
turnover
setback

7 **Work:** Key

— 2 —

b Here is a possible answer:

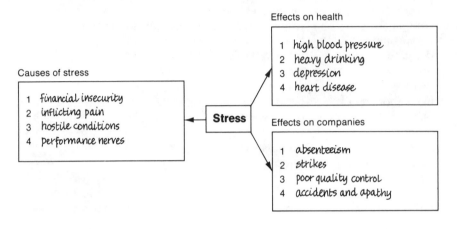

Causes of stress

1 financial insecurity
2 inflicting pain
3 hostile conditions
4 performance nerves

Stress

Effects on health

1 high blood pressure
2 heavy drinking
3 depression
4 heart disease

Effects on companies

1 absenteeism
2 strikes
3 poor quality control
4 accidents and apathy

— 3 —

a 1 m   2 f   3 n   4 k   5 h   6 i   7 b   8 a   9 j
10 g   11 e   12 d

SELF-STUDY ACTIVITIES

1 a) *a workaholic*: someone who cannot stop working – work is an addiction
  b) *a golden handshake*: a large sum of money given to someone (usually at management level) who has been made redundant
  c) *up to my eyes*: submerged – just as you might be standing in water which comes 'up to your eyes'. It normally refers to a lot of work which you have to do.
  d) *a high-flier*: someone with ability and ambition who will succeed in their chosen career (usually in a short time)
  e) *pull my socks up*: to change your ways and start working harder or more efficiently
  f) *a slave driver*: someone who makes you work very hard – not a pleasant boss

2 a) output   b) backlog   c) breakdown   d) setback
  e) turnover   f) downfall

8 Prepositions and phrases:
Teacher's notes

1

a 📼 With the possible exception of *fond, allergic* and *looking forward to*, the problem will not be meaning but the use of particular prepositions with these items. The main requirement therefore, is that the students get a lot of practice.

When the students have listened to the cassette and filled in the chart, they can compare their answers with a partner. You can then check their answers and provide further practice by asking the students to form questions which will elicit the answers, for example:
Sandra: Marcel, what is the man allergic to?
Marcel: I don't know the name exactly, but it's a type of penicillin.

b Ask the students to move round the class and interview other students, and make a note of any answers that they think are unusual. The class can then discuss the results and decide on the most unusual examples.

2

a Elicit the answers from the students when they have finished, and see if they are able to explain the meaning of each of the phrases. Explain any phrases they have not found.

b Follow the instructions in the Student Book.

c You can omit this activity if you are short of time, but it is good fun and does provide the students with an opportunity to put the phrases into contexts of their own creation.

3

a With the aid of dictionaries and the context, students are usually able to complete this exercise successfully; however, it is worth spending some extra time to clarify the differences between some of the target verbs. In particular, the difference between *accuse* and *blame* is very difficult for certain nationalities, and not easy to explain. If you accuse someone of something you are saying that you think they did something wrong or bad. If you blame someone for something, you are saying they are responsible for something which is wrong or bad. This need not mean the same thing: you could accuse a child of stealing apples, but blame the parents for bringing the child up badly.

b Explain the meaning of any new adjectives and then put the class into small groups for the discussion activity. You may wish to give an example: 'If someone mistook me for a pop star, I might be flattered or I might be annoyed. It would depend on who the pop star was.'

c This can be given for homework.

4

a There are too many concepts associated with these prepositions to include in a single exercise, but the diagrams can often help students with some of the most important concepts and you could begin by discussing the diagrams to see if the students are able to recognize the different concepts. Following that, they can do the exercise and discuss their answers with a partner. Check the answers at the end.

b Monitor the discussions carefully and help students with any problems.

SELF-STUDY ACTIVITIES

1 Follow the instructions in the Student Book.

2 Holiday photographs not only provide a generative context for the practice of 'dangling' prepositions, they can also form the basis of a very successful lesson with scope for discussion and further vocabulary expansion. The activity will also provide you with the ideal introduction to the next unit in the book.

3 Ask the students to bring their examples to class and then put the students in small groups. Together they can discuss their sentences and group them according to the different uses of *by*. If there are sufficient monolingual dictionaries in class, the students could then try to match their different groupings with the dictionary definitions.

8 Prepositions and phrases:
Key words and expressions

Verbs	Adjectives	Phrases
accuse sb. (of)	afraid (of)	at all
blame sb. (for)	allergic (to)	at first
congratulate sb. (on)	annoyed	at last
discourage sb. (from)	delighted	at least
introduce sb. (to)	flattered	at random
look forward to	fond (of)	by far
mistake sb. (for)	frustrated	by heart
prevent sb. (from)	good (at)	by the way
protect sb. (from)	grateful	in tears
remind sb. (of)	interested (in)	in the way
thank sb. (for)	jealous	on average
	puzzled	on earth
	relieved	on holiday
	shocked	on the way
	upset	
	worried (about)	

Other words and expressions

atlas	map
corridor	snakes
I'm thinking of -ing . . .	different uses of *at, on* and *in*

SELF-STUDY ACTIVITIES
---

all of a sudden	get married to sb.
at first glance	in the end
at the time	look after
complain about sth. or sb.	on second thoughts
for the time being	on the spur of the moment
from a distance	show sb. around

8 Prepositions and phrases: Key

1

a

	Man	*Woman*
Something you are . . .		
1 fond of	his two cats	swimming
2 interested in	playing in a brass band	fell walking
3 afraid of	death	snakes
4 worried about	where the next job is comming from	the same & being late
5 good at	playing his brass instrument	swimming
6 shocked by	tabloid newspapers	the same
7 allergic to	penicillin (called Vibramycin)	strawberries
8 looking forward to	going away after Christmas	going away at Christmas
9 thinking of doing fairly soon	visiting his sister	meeting a friend

2

a   at: first / all / last / random / least
    in: all / tears / the way
    on: earth / average / holiday / the way
    by: heart / far / the way

b   Here are some possible answers:
    1 There were <u>at least</u> forty people at the party.
    2 How <u>on earth</u> are you going to buy a Mercedes on your salary?
    3 We had to stop for petrol <u>on the way</u>.
    4 I learnt that poem <u>by heart</u> when I was at school.
    5 I visit my parents twice a week <u>on average</u>.
    6 It's <u>by far</u> the best record they've ever made.
    7 She enjoyed the film but I didn't like it <u>at all</u>.
    8 She broke down <u>in tears</u> when I gave her the news.

© Cambridge University Press 1991   ⟫→

9 The soldiers started firing into the crowd <u>at random</u>.
10 I found it quite difficult <u>at first</u> but I got used to it after a while.
11 We spent hours looking for somewhere to eat, and then <u>at last</u> we found a little restaurant that was open.
12 . . . lead a simple life. <u>By the way</u>, do you know what time it starts?

—— **3** ——————————————————————

a 1 c   2 g   3 e   4 h   5 i
6 b   7 a   8 j   9 f   10 d

b Possible answers are:
1 delighted / jealous
2 upset / frustrated / annoyed
3 upset / sad / annoyed / puzzled
4 delighted / relieved
5 delighted / flattered / annoyed
6 upset / annoyed / puzzled
7 grateful
8 upset / sad
9 annoyed
10 grateful / relieved

c 1 She congratulated me on winning.
2 She thanked me for carrying her suitcase.
3 She blamed me for losing the tickets.
4 She discouraged me from accepting the job.
5 She prevented me from leaving.
6 She accused me of not telling the truth.
7 She mistook me for the Prime Minister of Great Britain.
8 I reminded her of her niece.

—— **4** ——————————————————————

a 1 on, in   2 at, in   3 on, at   4 in, on   5 on, in
6 on, in   7 at, in   8 on, in   9 on, at   10 at, on, in

b 1 a) in a boat   b) for a swim
2 a) outside   b) inside
3 a) on one of the last pages   b) on the back cover
4 a) on short grass   b) in long grass
5 a) I pass it on my journey   b) it's an obstruction
6 a) inside   b) on top of the magazine
7 a) at work   b) in that room

SELF-STUDY ACTIVITIES

1 a) It was a terrible shock <u>at the time</u> but I soon got over it.
  b) It was a terrible journey but we got there <u>in the end</u>.
  c) I was tempted to jump off the cliff, but <u>on second thoughts</u> I decided it might be a bit dangerous.
  d) I hadn't made any plans: I just decided to go <u>on the spur of the moment</u>.
  e) I was driving along the motorway and then <u>all of a sudden</u> the engine just burst into flames.
  f) It looked like quite a nice restaurant <u>from a distance</u>, but when I got closer I realized it was just a cafe – and not very nice either.
  g) I thought it was going to be quite an easy exam <u>at first glance</u>, but in actual fact I found some of the questions very tricky.
  h) I've got a small dictionary which I can use <u>for the time being</u>, but I plan to buy a much better one when I start my new course.

2 a) with   b) at/in   c) to   d) around   e) to   f) after
  g) on   h) about

9 **Going places:** Teacher's notes

———— **1** ————————————————

a Students can do this activity in pairs, and should have access to dictionaries to look up new words, e.g. *zip, trolley, nappies*, etc. You can then check their answers and clarify any problems that have arisen.

b If you have a large class, i.e. over twenty, it would be wise to create more airport officials. This type of roleplay is usually quite chaotic (as are most airports), but it can be great fun and provides a lot of practice.

———— **2** ————————————————

a If you think your students will find this exercise difficult, you could do the first part with the whole class. Before the students work on their own you should also tell them that there may be more than one place in which they can insert the target words. For this reason, it is interesting for the students to compare their answers when they have finished.

b If your students do not go skiing, you could ask them to talk about holidays in general; this will still create an opportunity to use some of the vocabulary from **2a**.

———— **3** ————————————————

a Follow the instructions in the Student Book and allow the students to use dictionaries.

b When the students have compared their answers, you can check them and clarify any problems they had with new vocabulary before they attempt the gap-fill exercise.

c Explain the activity and then go through the list of words to make sure the students understand them. With the class you could then do a quick brainstorming activity to add more likely words and phrases to the list. The students can then build up an oral story in pairs, and finally tell their story to a pair who have worked on the alternative 'disaster' story. For further consolidation, they could write their stories for homework.

SELF-STUDY ACTIVITIES

1 If you wish, you could do the first part in class and then give the second part for self-study.

2 This task should enable students to build up a large set of descriptive adjectives and phrases, e.g. magnificent scenery, beautiful views, historic castles, miles of golden sand, etc. When they compare their answers in class they are also likely to discover that most students have recorded similar words and phrases, and this serves to demonstrate the likelihood of certain vocabulary appearing in particular types of text.

3 Check the answers to this exercise in class.

9 Going places:
Key words and expressions

Nouns		Verbs	Adjectives
boarding card	peak	collide (with)	antique
cargo vessel	resort	float	breathtaking
crash-landing	rope	hamper	bumpy
connection	runway	knock sth. off	challenging
escalator	slopes	modernize	charming
excess baggage	star sign	ram	dramatic
hand luggage	string	run out of sth.	elegant
harbour	trolley	scrape	full-scale
jetty	voyage	shiver	ideal
junction	X-ray	wrap sth. round	luxury
label	yacht		original
mast	zip		picturesque
			reasonably-priced

Other words and expressions

double room or twin-bedded room
en route
run aground
to be situated (on the coast)
to get stuck

SELF-STUDY ACTIVITIES
---

canal	boarding card / landing card
desert	charter flight / scheduled flight
falls	day trip / business trip
forest	full board / half board
island	package tour / sightseeing tour
jungle	sand beach / pebbly beach
ocean	standby ticket / return ticket
pass	tourist resort / ski resort

9 **Going places:** Key

1
---

a 1 1   4   6   11   12   13   17   18
2 Probable answers are: a) 7   8   11   14   16   18   19
    b) 6   7   8   10   11   12   13
3 routine: 1   2   3   4   6   8   9   11   12   13   14   15   16   17
       18   19
   unusual: 5   7   10   20

2
---

a Here are some possible answers:

Champery:

ideally situated
traditional resort / aspects
dramatic peaks
picturesque: Val d'Illiez / resort / valley / Swiss alpine village

Accommodation:

beautiful: three-storey chalet / pine walls / village / surrounding
   countryside / Swiss farmhouse / features / pine furniture
luxury: three-storey chalet / bathrooms / Swiss farmhouse / shower room
antique: open fireplace / pine furniture
elegant: open fireplace / pine furniture / features
successfully retained
breathtaking views
original: pine walls / open fireplace / cast iron wood-burning stove / charm
charming: three-storey chalet / Swiss farmhouse / village / features

Skiing in Champery:

challenging: runs / World Cup Downhill
ideal starting point
gentle slopes of Planachaux
reasonably-priced ski pass

—— **3** ——————————————————————————

a boats and sailing:
 voyage   sailed   harbour   jetty   ran aground
 off the coast   sand banks   harbour   floating
 yacht   trimaran   ropes   cargo vessel   mast

 hitting:
 rammed   ran aground   scraped
 collided (with)   hit   knocked

b 1 collided   5 stuck
   2 hampered   6 en route
   3 wrapped   7 floating
   4 full-scale   8 scrape

—————| **SELF-STUDY ACTIVITIES** |—————————

1 Sahara Desert   Panama Canal   Atlantic Ocean   Khyber Pass
  Mount Everest   Niagara Falls   Canary Islands   Amazon Jungle
  The Black Forest   Lake Michigan

3 a) flight   e) trip
  b) ticket   f) resort
  c) card   g) board
  d) tour   h) beach

10 **Affixation:** Teacher's notes

1

---

a Allow students to use dictionaries to help them. When you check the answers pay special attention to the pronunciation of some items. For example, you could point out that -*ate* is almost always pronounced /eɪt/ at the end of verbs, but /ət/ at the end of adjectives. Other words that cause problems are *unhygienic* /ʌnhaɪdʒ:inɪk/ and *unsuccessful* /ʌnsəksesfəl/. If you teach German speakers you should also point out that the prefix is not normally stressed in English.

b Be sure to emphasize that the general pattern emerging is a pattern and not a rule. It is unlikely, however, that your students will be able to think of many exceptions; you could give them some examples from the key.

c This activity provides further practice but is also likely to highlight conceptual problems that students are not fully aware of, e.g. *accurate* does not have a one-to-one equivalent in many other languages, and students may wish to talk about an 'inaccurate bus service', which would not be possible in English. (We would describe a service as *infrequent* or *unreliable*.)

2

---

a Follow the instructions in the Student Book and then check the answers. Repeat the procedure for **b**.

c ⬛ Stop the tape after each example to give your students time to write down their answers. If they are finding it difficult, play the tape twice. Ask the students to compare their answers before you check them with the whole class.

3

---

a If you monitor the group discussions, you will probably discover the words which are not fully understood by the students, and this will then lead to some discussion with the group as a whole.

b This is a testing exercise rather than a practice activity, but you could provide further practice with the following game:

Read out the adjectives and ask the students to write down a noun which might logically follow, e.g. *classical + composer, economic + problem, various + jobs* and so on. Two adjectives you cannot use in this activity are *alive* and *alone*, as these form part of a small group of adjectives which cannot precede a noun (*ill* and *asleep* fall into the same category). When you have finished, the students should cover the adjectives and then show a partner their list of nouns; the partner has to try and guess the adjective which preceded it.

SELF-STUDY ACTIVITIES

1 If you wish, you could use this as a 'warmer' activity at the beginning of a lesson: it is a very simple mechanism for getting students to hunt through their own mental lexicon, and it is surprising the number of correct words that students can sometimes generate from using their imagination coupled with intelligent guesswork, e.g. unworkable, unreadable, unforgivable, etc.

2 Students can check their answers with a dictionary or the Word-building tables at the back of the Student Book.

3 If your students do not have their own copies of the book, you could do this activity in class.

10 Affixation:
Key words and expressions

Adjectives

alone / lonely	(in)flexible
bored / boring	(in)frequent
childish / childlike	live / alive / living
classic / classical	terrific / terrifying
dead / deadly / deathly	(un)democratic
economic / economical	(un)faithful
imaginative / imaginary	(un)fashionable
(in)accurate	(un)forgivable
(in)appropriate	(un)helpful
(in)compatible	(un)hygienic
(in)comprehensible	(un)predictable
(in)convenient	(un)scientific
(in)efficient	(un)successful
	various / varied

Verbs

misbehave
misjudge
mislead
mispronounce
overcharge
overreact
oversleep
overspend
redesign
re-elect
re-examine
reopen
undress
unfold
unlock
unscrew
untie
unwrap

Other words and expressions

award	dreary	novel/novelist
best friend	experiment	pair of jeans
composer	married couple	sarcastic

SELF-STUDY ACTIVITIES

advise / advice
advocate
commute / commuting *and* commuter
conflict
contradict / contradiction
contribute / contribution
demonstrate / demonstration
elect / election
execute / execution
hesitate / hesitation

illustrate / illustration
persecute / persecution
predict / prediction
protect / protection
reject / rejection
respect
revise / revision
restrict / restriction
supervise / supervision
televise / television

10 Affixation: Key

a

	-able	-ible	-ful	-ent	-ic	-ate
un-	uncomfortable unfashionable unforgivable unpredictable		unfaithful unsuccessful unhelpful		unscientific unhygienic undemocratic	
in-		inflexible incomprehensible incompatible		infrequent incompetent inefficient inconvenient		inappropriate inaccurate

b The general pattern is:
un- is used with the suffixes *-able*, *-ful*, and *-ic*.
in- is used with the suffixes *-ible*, *-ent*, and *-ate*.
Exceptions include: *unfortunate, inconceivable* and *inexplicable*.

c Here are some possible answers:
a watch: inaccurate
a married couple: incompatible
your best friend: this depends on your friend
a pair of jeans: uncomfortable / unfashionable
a political leader: unpredictable / inflexible
a meeting at 2.30 p.m.: inconvenient
a cracked cup: unhygienic
a company: unsuccessful / inefficient
an experiment: unscientific / unsuccessful
a society: undemocratic
an old car: uncomfortable / unpredictable
a poem: incomprehensible
someone's behaviour: unforgivable
a bus service: inefficient / infrequent
a married man or woman: unfaithful

─── **2** ───

a

Prefix	Examples	Meaning
un-	unlock unfold	to reverse an action/process
re-	rewrite rebuild	to do something again
over-	overeat overdo	to do something too much
mis-	misunderstand misread	to do something badly/ incorrectly

b oversleep   reopen   untie   re-elect   re-examine
misbehave   unscrew   overcharge   redesign   misjudge
overspend   undress   mislead   unwrap / rewrap
mispronounce

c

1 The man probably overslept and his boss overreacted.
2 Mathew misbehaved and started unwrapping the presents.
3 They misjudged him; he has overspent.
4 The committee misled them and they have re-elected Hopkins.
5 He had to undress again so they could re-examine him.

─── **3** ───

a *bored* is used to describe how a person feels
boring is used to describe the thing/event which causes the feeling

economic refers to the economy of a country or a company
economical simply means that something does not require a lot of money or effort

live means 'not recorded – happening at this moment' often in front of an audience (of a TV programme or concert, for example); also used for wires etc. which have electricity running through them
alive is the opposite of *dead* but cannot be used before a noun
living means the same as *alive* but is used before a noun

classic means a very good example of something, e.g. a book or a film
classical usually refers to music or architecture which has a traditional form

childish is used as a criticism of immature behaviour
childlike refers to someone's appearance etc. which is like a child's but it is not intended to be a criticism

dead means the opposite of *alive / living*
deadly usually describes a weapon which can kill
deathly means that something makes you think of death, e.g., someone with no colour in their face

alone simply means there is nobody with you
lonely suggests that you would like to be with other people or that a place makes you feel like this

terrific means wonderful
terrifying means very frightening

imaginative refers to someone with a lot of imagination – a lot of ideas
imaginary refers to something which only exists in your imagination – something which is not real

various means several – a number of
varied refers to things which are different from each other – not all the same

b living   dead   live   boring   terrific   economical
    varied   imaginative   alone   deadly   childish   classical

---

SELF-STUDY ACTIVITIES

1 Examples include:
  unforgivable   unforgettable   unreadable   unreliable
  undeniable   unbreakable   unbelievable   unbearable
  unreasonable   unavoidable   unfavourable   unworkable

2 advise (advice is the noun)
  conflict (conflict, with the stress on the first syllable, is the noun)
  respect (respect is the noun and has the same stress as the verb)
  commute (commuting/commuter are the nouns)
  advocate (advocate (= lawyer) is the noun)

11 Is it right?: Teacher's notes

1

a Give your students ten minutes, and see if they can complete the exercise with the use of dictionaries and from the context. Check the answers and clarify any problems.

b Encourage the students to try and think of situations in which different words from **1a** could be used with a positive and negative meaning, e.g. *objective* may be used positively to suggest that someone is fair and shows no favouritism but it may be used negatively to suggest that someone is always cold, detached, and lacking in human warmth.

2

a Parallel texts on a common theme not only allow students to see target items contextualized in different ways, they also provide an opportunity for controlled practice which is both motivating and generative. In this case, students read different texts, and before they pair up to exchange stories you might ask each student to check their answers with someone who has worked on the same story; this provides each student with a 'dry run' before they tell their story to someone who hasn't read it. You might also tell the students to cover the text they are not reading; this eliminates the possibility of students reading both stories.

b In my experience, the exchange of stories often leads on quite naturally to a discussion of the 'rights' and 'wrongs' in each story; if this happens, let the discussions continue, and omit **2b** as a separate activity.

3

a Put the students in groups of three and allow them to use dictionaries to help them. After about ten minutes, check their understanding of the words and clarify any problems.

b In the same groups, see if they can construct a possible story using all of the words and phrases. At the end, listen to two or three stories with the whole class and ask them to vote on the one which they think is nearest to the story they are about to read. Now let them read the story. If you think some students might read the story before this point, write the target items on the board rather than allow the students to use their books.

d This can be omitted if you are short of time, or feel you have exhausted the subject.

SELF-STUDY ACTIVITIES

1 These are all common student errors, so check the answers in class in a future lesson.

2 This is usually more successful with groups who have an interest in politics as political news stories are full of bias and prejudice of one sort or another.

3 In this exercise, students are exploiting the lexical relationship of antonymy to lead them to the correct answer, e.g. admit ≠ deny, condemn ≠ condone, and so on. Do the first question in class to illustrate this point, and ask them to complete it for homework. Check the answers in a future lesson.

11 Is it right?:
Key words and expressions

Nouns

addiction
blood test
court case
discrimination
heart attack
jury
manslaughter
maternity ward
mix-up
motive
nursery
row
suspended sentence
victim

Verbs

adopt (a child)
assault
beat sb. up
blame
bring up (a child)
deny
disrupt
humiliate
reveal
stab
strangle

Adjectives

biased
distraught
egalitarian
foolproof
(il)legal
neutral
objective
one-sided
pregnant
prejudiced
subjective
(un)fair

Other words and expressions

be entitled to something
be given custody
commit suicide
give birth

racial prejudice
regain consciousness
throughout

SELF-STUDY ACTIVITIES

according to (sb. or sth.)
check (a passport)
condemn
condone
conform
deny + -ing
detain

disguise
feel sorry for sb.
ignore
knowledge (of sth.)
prosecute
provoke
rebel

release
retaliate
surrender
tighten (up)
to do a course
you're not allowed to

11 Is it right?: Key

a 1 fair
   2 one-sided
   3 biased
   4 reasonable
   5 subjective   objective

   6 neutral
   7 prejudiced
   8 balanced
   9 egalitarian
  10 unfair

b

Positive words	Negative words	Positive or negative
fair balanced egalitarian reasonable	unfair biased prejudiced	subjective objective neutral one-sided

─── 2 ───

a

	Text A	Text B
The victim	Mrs Margaret Burton	Dominic Sparkes
The accused	Mr Frederick Burton	Julie Flores
The crime	manslaughter	manslaughter
The cause(s) of death	strangulation/heart attack	hit on the head & stabbed
The motive(s)	anger	anger over what he had done to her daughter
The sentence	9-month suspended sentence	2-year suspended sentence
The reason for the light sentence	no intention to kill and considerable provocation	diminished responsibility because he had made her daughter pregnant, beaten her up etc.

SELF-STUDY ACTIVITIES
---

1 a) <u>You are</u> not allowed to smoke in theatres in England.
  b) My knowledge <u>of</u> the legal system is very poor.
  c) I went to England to do a <u>course</u> in Constitutional Law.
  d) She denied <u>starting</u> the fire.
  e) In _____ most countries it is illegal to drive without insurance.
  f) The officials will <u>check</u> your passport at the border.
  g) When parents separate I feel sorry <u>for</u> the children.
  h) She tried to <u>commit</u> suicide.
  i) In my opinion <u>rapists</u> should go to prison for at least ten years.
  j) You can be <u>prosecuted</u> if you trespass on someone's property.

3 a) denied   f) ignored
  b) conform   g) got away
  c) condemn   h) released
  d) surrendered   i) recognized
  e) retaliated   j) tighten up

12 Revision and expansion:
Teacher's notes

1

Some of these verbs collocate with a restricted number of nouns, e.g.
commit, while others may combine with a wide range of nouns, e.g. *lend*.
When the students have finished, they can move round the class and
compare answers.

2

Places such as hospitals, schools and prisons trigger off different
associations for different people, so there is no correct answer to this
exercise. Again, the students can compare their maps and explain why they
have positioned words in particular places. This type of subjective
organization of vocabulary is a very powerful memory aid.

3

Follow the instructions in the Student Book and make sure your students are
able to justify each of their answers.

4

Follow the instructions in the Student Book.

5

Follow the instructions in the Student Book. Pronunciation exercises are a
good way to revise vocabulary, and vice versa.

6

This activity draws on vocabulary from Unit 9 but it is also an opportunity
for the students to revise additional lexical items within this topic. You
could ask students to complete the network individually and then consider

ways of extending it with a partner. At the end, pairs can compare their answers.

—— **7** ——————————————————————————

If you haven't done all the exercises which are being tested here, you could write your own quiz based on units and exercises you have covered. It is a very simple way of revising a great deal of vocabulary in a single exercise.

—— **8** ——————————————————————————

Students could do this orally in class or write their stories for homework.

—— **9** ——————————————————————————

This type of brainstorming activity is more fun if you put the students in pairs and then impose a strict time limit.

—— **10** ——————————————————————————

You can make this game more competitive and challenging by telling students that they score one point for each correct sentence, but if they include another person's preposition in their sentence, then the other person also scores a point.

—— **11** ——————————————————————————

Follow the instructions in the Student Book.

—— **12** ——————————————————————————

This activity not only revises a wide range of vocabulary, it also provides valuable practice in paraphrasing and defining vocabulary items. Some teachers may be worried that students will simply pass on their mistakes and misunderstandings, but we believe it is important for students to take responsibility of this sort, and it can contribute to a more supportive classroom environment which can greatly facilitate effective learning.

12 Revision and expansion:
New words and expressions

glance (at)
poison
run out of sth.
wallet

12 Revision and expansion: Key

───── **1** ─────────────────────────────

Here are some possible answers:
1 Teachers spend hours marking homework.
2 Criminals commit crimes.
3 Dealers buy and sell shares.
4 Parents bring up children.
5 Judges sentence criminals.
6 People elect governments.
7 Banks lend money.
8 People obey orders.
9 Employers recruit staff.
10 People cancel appointments.

───── **3** ─────────────────────────────

Here are some possible answers:
1 *threaten someone*: this does not involve physical violence
2 *poison someone*: this does not involve a violent attack – it's invisible
3 *tiring*: this is a negative idea
4 *luxury*: this is not related to the past
5 *be promoted*: all the others involve leaving your company
6 *vet*: all the others use words/speech to do their job

───── **4** ─────────────────────────────

Here are some likely answers:
1 thinking   2 afraid   3 interested   4 looking forward
5 shocked   6 good   7 allergic   8 fond   9 worried
10 run out

© Cambridge University Press 1991

5

○ ○	○ ○
voyage	canal
channel	dessert
desert	commute
average	antique
cottage	resort
hazard	hotel
addict	collide
	recruit

6

Here is an example of a completed network.

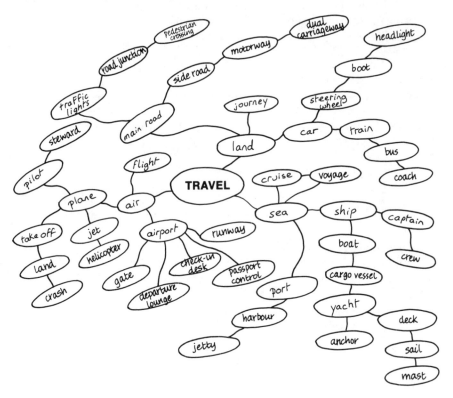

—— 7 ——

Refer to the relevant pages in the Student Book for answers.

—— 9 ——

Refer to the word-building tables at the back of the Student Book for answers.

—— 10 ——

Here are the likely combinations:

at: at first   at all   look at   at random   glance at   at least
good at   at last   at the end

on: on holiday   on the way   take on   on earth
on time   congratulate sb. on   on strike   on the outskirts of

of: accuse sb. of   all of a sudden   remind sb. of   run out of
lack of   on the outskirts of   out of date

for: apologize for   look for   blame sb. for   thank sb. for
mistake sb. for

—— 11 ——

Refer to page 29 in the Student Book for possible answers.

13 **Newspapers:** Teacher's notes

1

a This may appear more relevant to students learning in England, but we have found most adult learners are keen to discover the similarities and differences between newspapers in England and their own country. If possible, take a selection of English papers into the classroom; students can look through them as a way of checking their answers to **1a**.

b When the students have read the second part of the text, go through the example carefully before the students work on the sentences that have to be modified.

c This part is clearly more suitable for a mixed nationality class, although students from the same country do not always share the same opinion of their newspapers.

2

a You may wish to illustrate the point by doing one example with the class, e.g. *Amnesty alleges mass state killings*. In the article, this information is paraphrased and/or expanded in the following way:

Amnesty = Amnesty International
alleges = says
mass = tens of thousands
state = government agents

At the end, check the answers and clarify any problems.

b This could be done in pairs or groups.

c As this activity is quite time-consuming, you could restrict the number of opening sentences for each group, or give the activity for homework.

3

a Follow the instructions in the Student Book, and ask the students to compare their answers when they have finished. Check with the whole class.

b   This is suitable as a homework activity.

SELF-STUDY ACTIVITIES

1 This is rather a long rubric, complicated by the fact that the learning environment – an English speaking country or the learner's own country – will affect the approach taken. It would be wise therefore, to go through the rubric with the students, and try to motivate them to carry out the task. You could have a feedback session in a future lesson. Inevitably, this type of learning strategy will not appeal to everyone, but if it provides an effective long-term strategy for just one student, it has been worthwhile.

2 For students who are interested in vocabulary commonly found in headlines, this provides a further opportunity for them to expand their knowledge.

3 This is a fun activity and you could ask your students to try and find their own examples of typographical errors from an English newspaper and bring them to class. This activity is more practical for students who are studying in an English speaking country with ready access to a range of papers in English.

13 Newspapers:
Key words and expressions

Nouns

ambulance	pledge	
bias	public opinion	
blast	restriction	
cartoon	review	
chaos	spokesman	
corruption	stock market	
crew	subsidy	
dispute	talks	
gossip column	trade union/union	
overtime	warehouse	
pay rise	weather forecast	
pin-up	work-to-rule	

Verbs

allege
break down
claim
criticize
curb
drop
glamorize
launch
pledge
pry (into)
quit
step up
urge
worsen

Other words and expressions

aimed at	popular press / tabloids
in support of	quality press
it is often said that . . .	right-wing
largely	tend to . . .
left-wing	to a large / certain extent
on standby	X is regarded as . . .

SELF-STUDY ACTIVITIES

Headline words:

back = support	scare = fear
gap = difference	split = divided
held = detained	threat = danger
key = important	

13 Newspapers: Key

1
---

a You are likely to find in a quality paper in Great Britain: theatre reviews, cartoons, overseas news, adverts for BMW cars, weather forecast and stock market prices.
You are likely to find in a popular paper: gossip column, cartoons, adverts for self-assembly kitchen units, weather forecast and pin-ups.

b Here are some possible answers:
1 Television tends to glamorize violence.
   It is often said that television glamorizes violence.
2 She claims to be a communist.
   She is regarded by some people as a communist.
3 All newspapers tend to be biased.
   All newspapers are sometimes criticized for being biased.
4 It claims to be a democratic country.
   It's a democratic country to a certain extent.
5 People largely believe what they read in newspapers.
   People believe what they read in newspapers to a large extent.
6 Expensive clothes are regarded by some people as a status symbol.
   Expensive clothes are largely a status symbol.

2
---

a 1a   2h   3b   4c   5e   6d   7f   8g

3
---

a Ambulance staff step up pay action
para. 1: stepped up   para. 3: leaders, emergency
para. 4: talks, dispute, the army

Ambulance chaos set to worsen
para. 1: worsen   para. 2: union   para. 3: restrictions
para. 4: stand-by, broke down   para. 5: called in

SELF-STUDY ACTIVITIES

2 backs = supports   threat = danger   held = detained
   split = divided   scare = fear   gap = difference

3 a) *died* should be *dived*   d) *soap* should be *soup*
   b) *kitchen* should be *kitten*   e) *choir* should be *chair*
   c) *blind* should be *blond*   f) *eating* should be *beating*

14 Verbs: Teacher's notes

1
---

a If your students cannot find the answer, give them a clue, e.g. the answer is connected with grammar. At the end explain any new verbs, e.g. *breed, bet, mend, blink* and *stink.*

b Follow the instructions in the Student Book.

2
---

a Go through the answers when the students have finished, but don't explain why the underlined verbs are wrong at this stage.

b Now see if the students can correct each of the sentences using the underlined verbs. In actual fact, the students should be able to find the correct answer by looking through the different sentences (the underlined verbs are all used correctly in one or more of the sentences).

c Verb patterns are a common source of error, so it is important that the students keep a record of verbs which take particular constructions. You could ask them to note down each of the patterns, e.g. verb + object + infinitive, and then, in pairs or groups, to write down all the verbs they can think of which take this pattern. If your students want further practice, you will find several suitable activities in *A Way with Words Book 2*, Unit 17.

3
---

a Check the answers with the class and clarify the meaning of any new words.

b Follow the instructions in the Student Book and help students with any new language.

c 📼 Play the tape once and ask the students to compare their answers with a partner. If there is any disagreement, play the tape a second time.

d The students will now have a framework for their own story, but you
could brainstorm the task with the class for a few minutes to give them
more ideas. In our experience students have often chosen to set the story
around a drug smuggling ring, a night club or big business. When the
students have generated a few ideas they can work on their stories,
individually or in groups, and they should be encouraged to use
vocabulary from **3a**. At the end they can read their stories to other
students, or better still, record their stories for homework and then
exchange cassettes.

4

a With the exception of *spread*, you can demonstrate the literal meaning of
the other verbs in class. Do this to check understanding, and then see if
the students can complete the exercise. Check the answers at the end.
If you have a monolingual group, it might be interesting to see if the
translation equivalents can also be used with these different meanings.

b Encourage the students to look for ways to incorporate the different
verbs into these stories. Inevitably, this will lead to a few mistakes, but it
is important that students experiment with new language, and from their
mistakes they are likely to develop a better understanding of how these
verbs can be used.

SELF-STUDY ACTIVITIES

1 Even at this level students still make mistakes with irregular verbs, and as a
test administered by the students themselves, it is more fun. You may also be
surprised by the number of new words the students learn through such an
exercise.

2 Check the answers in class in a future lesson.

3 In their desire to learn 'new' words, students sometimes do not
appreciate the importance of learning different meanings of familiar
verbs, and less common meanings of verbs such as *leave* and *see* are
often overlooked.
   If your students do not have access to good monolingual dictionaries,
you could do this exercise in class and just concentrate on the translation
equivalents in the students' mother tongue.

14 Verbs:
Key words and expressions

Verbs

bend	point out
bet	release
bleed	seduce
blink	sink
blow	smuggle
breed	spread
crawl	stick
feed	stink
flash	surrender
go away	tease
grab	turn up (=arrive)
mend	upset

Verb patterns

advise
beg
encourage ⎫ + object + full infinitive
persuade
want

insist
propose ⎫ + that . . .
suggest

enjoy
loathe
mind ⎫ + -ing
regret
remember

let ⎫ + object + bare infinitive
make

expect ⎫ + full infinitive
hope

Other words and expressions

come to a head	I'm used to -ing . . .	rumour
fall asleep	jump the queue	slip through
fall in love	leave me alone	to give oneself up
get into a fight	let me go	(£5) doesn't go far these
gypsy	make fun of sb.	days
I'm thinking of -ing . . .	reach a climax	

SELF-STUDY ACTIVITIES

---

book sb. sth.	owe sb. sth.
cash sb. sth.	pour sb. sth.
lend sb. sth.	save sb. sth.
offer sb. sth.	throw sb. sth.

14 Verbs: Key

1

a The answers are all related to verb forms:
- *need* is regular; the other verbs are all irregular.
- the past tense and past participle of *get* is *got*; the other verbs keep the same form for past tense and past participle. (In some dictionaries, an alternative form *betted* is given, but this is extremely rare.)
- *mend* is regular; the other verbs are irregular.
- *blink* is regular; the other verbs are irregular.
- the past tense of *show* is regular, the other verbs are irregular.

b Here are some possible answers:

I breed horses.	I bet £5 on that race.
I had to feed the baby.	The wind blew the tree down.
The ship sank.	I can't bend my knee.
I lent her £5.	I expect those socks stink.

2

a/b Here are the underlined words from **2a** put into correct sentences.
1 He suggested that we go to a Chinese restaurant.
2 She insisted that I take the exam.
3 He made us leave.
4 I don't expect to see them.
5 I agreed to work with him.
6 She wanted me to move the furniture.
7 I am thinking of starting work after the holidays.
8 They wanted me to stay at their house.
9 He told me that it was very dangerous.
10 I'm hoping to work with him.

c 1 verb + *that* clause
2 verb + object + bare infinitive
3 verb + full infinitive
4 verb + object + full infinitive
5 verb + preposition + -ing form
6 verb + -ing form
7 verb + object + *that* clause

──── **3** ────────────────

a look for/try to find   reach a climax/come to a head
stab someone/attack someone with a knife   arrive/turn up
give oneself up/surrender   let me go/release me
leave me alone/go away

c [cassette] These are the most obvious differences:

Text	*Recording*
1 he let her go	she escaped
2 she seduces him	she teases and makes fun of him
3 he stabs her	she stabs him

──── **4** ────────────────

a 1c   2e   3d   4b   5g   6a   7h   8f

──── **SELF-STUDY ACTIVITIES** ────────

2 Here are some possible answers:
a) She lent me £5.
b) He poured me a glass of wine.
c) I owe him £10.
d) She saved me a seat.
e) She cashed me a cheque.
f) He booked me a flight.
g) They offered me money.
h) He threw me a box of matches.

3 a) find out   b) accompany   c) witness   d) picture
e) make sure   f) understand

© Cambridge University Press 1991

15 **Choices:** Teacher's notes

1
---

a Go through the list of expressions, adding more examples as you proceed:
I'd much prefer *Spain* to *Italy*.
I'd prefer to *live in Spain*.
The students should not have any problems with the meaning of these expressions, but they often need practice in making them part of their active vocabulary.

b Tell the students to read through the choices to make sure they understand the vocabulary. They can then work on the activity in groups, using the expressions from **1a** and also giving reasons for their preferences.

2
---

a The students may prefer to do this activity in pairs, and they should have access to dictionaries to find out / check their answers. You can go through the questions with the class at the end, and you can also highlight key expressions on the board:
We're not sure
We can't make up our minds $\Big\}$ whether to . . . or . . .
We haven't decided yet
We are thinking of . . . Alternatively, we might just . . .

b This activity is usually more interesting with a mixed nationality group as it uncovers a number of cultural differences. Before the students start, remind them of the expressions from **1a**; they will need them here.

c Students often uncover these words in the process of doing **2a**; if so, omit it.

3
---

a See how many phrases or sentences the students are able to generate using these verbs. You can, in fact, do this as a brainstorming activity with the class as a whole, writing the examples on the board.

b ▭ It is unlikely that a student on their own will have time to write down all the answers, so you could ask students to work in groups of three: one student concentrates on *catch* and *take*; one concentrates on *run* and *work out*; and one on *get*. When the students have listened to the tape they can discuss their answers and complete **3c**.

d/e These allow for freer practice; follow the instructions in the Student Book.

SELF-STUDY ACTIVITIES

1 This extends the vocabulary from exercise **2** of the unit by adding adjectives which commonly combine with the nouns, e.g. velvet curtains. You can check the answers in class and can also consolidate the vocabulary through student dialogues, for example:

A: Have you got a garden?
B: Yeah.
A: Is it quite sheltered?
B: Yes it is.
A: And have you got high ceilings in your house?
B: No, not particularly.

And so on.

2 Once again, students can compare and discuss their answers in a future lesson if you feel the subject will interest most of the class.

3 Remember to follow up this activity in class. It would be very easy for students to read through these ideas and then forget all about them; with a little persistence on your part, these strategies will be used by some students to great effect.

15 Choices:
Key words and expressions

Nouns

		Verbs
alcove	injection	dig
attic	lawn	hang around
basement	loft	prosecute
blinds	patio	put up (a picture)
cellar	rug	run: buses run every ten minutes
conservatory	rushhour	it's expensive to run a car
dishwasher	shelves	varnish
fence	sofa-bed	work sth. out
filling	terrace	
fireplace	tile	
flower bed	wallpaper	
hedge		

Other words and expressions

alternatively
a row of (shops)
handy (= convenient)
I don't think there's much to
 choose between them
I'd prefer to . . .
I'd rather . . .
If I had the choice, I'd go for . . .
I'm not sure whether to . . . or . . .
I prefer X to Y

it works out at (£5 each)
make up one's mind
monolingual / bilingual
on the outskirts of
overlooking
supposed to
take a short cut
(they don't) take any notice of
 (cyclists)
you're not meant to

SELF-STUDY ACTIVITIES

acceleration	furnished flat / house	reputation
concrete floor	high ceiling	sheltered garden
damp cellar	image	terraced house
depreciation	iron gate	velvet curtains
fitted carpet / kitchen	patterned wallpaper / curtains	

15 Choices: Key

2

a 1 rugs   2 blinds   3 wallpaper   4 shelves   5 tiles
6 wardrobe   7 sofa   8 patio   9 lawn   10 fence

c The other words are: basement, cellar, terrace, balcony, loft.

3

b 🔲 The verbs are used in the following phrases on the tape:
1 I can <u>get</u> the bus . . . which <u>takes</u> me to . . .
2 . . . how long does it <u>take</u>?
3 They're supposed to <u>run</u> every five minutes . . .
4 I <u>get</u> off at . . .
5 . . . if you <u>get</u> a monthly travel card . . .
6 . . . it <u>works out</u> at about a pound a day.
7 Why <u>don't</u> you <u>take</u> the car?
8 . . . the traffic's <u>been</u> <u>getting</u> really bad – if you <u>get</u> stuck in . . .
9 I can <u>take</u> a short cut through . . .
10 . . . if they <u>catch</u> you it's a twenty-five pound fine.
11 Most drivers <u>don't take</u> any notice of cyclists . . .
12 . . . the quickest way to <u>get</u> to work.

c 🔲

	Advantages	Disadvantages
by bus	handy, cheap, sometimes quick	unreliable service
by tube	generally a bit quicker than the bus	more expensive, not as convenient
by car	good if the weather is bad, you can stop for shopping	can take a long time because of traffic, can be stressful.
by bike	quickest way to get to work, cheapest	can be dangerous, can be unpleasant in winter

SELF-STUDY ACTIVITIES

1 furnished house / flat   patterned curtains / wallpaper
  high ceiling   velvet curtains
  damp house / cellar / flat   terraced house
  iron gate   fitted kitchen
  sheltered garden   concrete floor

16 Connecting words and ideas:
Teacher's notes

1

---

a Follow the instructions in the Student Book. When the students have finished they can compare and discuss their answers before you check them with the class.

b This activity consolidates vocabulary from **1a**. It also highlights the fact that a choice of link words may be available in a given situation, but that different sentence constructions may be required to accommodate these alternative words.

c Several of these link words, e.g. *moreover* and *however*, are commonly used at the beginning of a sentence to introduce an addition to or contrast with the previous sentence; this means the students will need to produce two sentences in order to contextualize these words. Make this clear to them before they start.
For further practice see exercise 2 in the *Self-study activities*.

2

---

a Students should be familiar with many of these words but they rarely use them; and when they do they often get them wrong. See if the students can complete the exercise on their own without any pre-teaching. When they have finished they can discuss their answers with a partner and then you can check the answers with the class.

b This activity often demonstrates a feature of vocabulary learning: students may appear to understand the meaning of a word but using it productively is another matter. You will almost certainly find that students uncover problems with these words when they try to incorporate them into their own contexts. For this reason you will probably need to monitor their efforts and be prepared to help with further explanations.

3

---

a *Lunch* and *dinner* are both hyponyms of the superordinate *meal*, i.e. they are specific examples of a more general type. In the same way, *hammer* and *screwdriver* are hyponyms of the superordinate *tool*. This lexical relationship is commonly employed as a linking device in conversation, and the exercise teaches and practises lexical items through this common feature of discourse.

Put the students in pairs and see how many answers they can provide without looking at the box of words at the end of the unit; they should refer to it when they have done as much as they can. Move round the class checking their different sentences, and when you are satisfied with the answers move on to **3b**. You may wish to change the pairs for this second activity.

—— **4** ——

a The target items in this exercise are commonly used as linking devices to refer to ideas mentioned elsewhere in a written or spoken text, but they are rarely taught in English language coursebooks and students are often very reluctant to try and use them.

Go through the examples very carefully to make sure the students are clear about the function of these words. When you are satisfied, they can try **4b** and then compare their answers in pairs or groups.

—— | SELF-STUDY ACTIVITIES | ——

1 In order to answer these questions the students may need to do a bit of vocabulary research of their own. This can be done at home so that you can maximize class time for productive practice.

2 You should check the answers to this exercise in class as it is important to mention that these phrases act as synonyms for the link words in **1a**, but that there is sometimes a difference in style: the link words here are generally more informal than those appearing in the text in **1a**. The distinction is not rigid, but it would be less common to find these link words in a piece of formal writing.

3 Check the findings in class. If you feel it has been a worthwhile exercise, you could repeat it at regular intervals.

16 Connecting words and ideas:
Key words and phrases

Nouns		**Adverbs**	**Link words/phrases**
ant	loyalty	apparently	although
approach	material	eventually	however
aspect	meal	generally	in spite of
belongings	measures	hopefully	in view of (the
circumstances	outcome	ideally	fact that)
cockroach	pets	luckily	moreover
crops	profit (≠ loss)	originally	of course
dilemma	proposal	potentially	provided (that)
enthusiasm	rate	presumably	unless
equipment	resources	recently	yet
expenses	scheme		
facilities	screwdriver		
filing cabinet	tent		
hammer	tools		
insects	torch		
issue	weapons		
	wheat		
	working conditions		

Other words and expressions

anger (v)
antagonize
bring sth. to a complete standstill
minimize
overall

retail
tackle (an issue/a problem)
to be faced with (a problem)
widen

SELF-STUDY ACTIVITIES

as long as
considering that

despite
in addition

needless to say

16   Connecting words and ideas: Key

—— 1 ——

a   in spite of   in view of the fact that   moreover
   however   provided (that)   of course

b   The changes necessary in order to use the other phrases are:
   . . . <u>although</u> market conditions have been difficult.
   . . . <u>in view of</u> the high level of interest rates throughout the year.
   . . . <u>unless</u> we are unable to / cannot complete . . .

c   Here are some possible answers:
   1   <u>Although</u> she worked hard, she still failed the exam.
   2   She passed the exam <u>in spite of</u> her illness.
   3   She was surprised to pass the exam <u>in view of the fact that</u> she hadn't
      done any work for it.
   4   She passed the exam. <u>Moreover</u>, she was awarded a scholarship as a
      result. <u>However</u>, she later discovered there had been a mistake and she
      had failed the exam.
   5   She thought she could pass the exam <u>provided that</u> she worked hard.
   6   <u>In view of</u> her long illness, she is unlikely to do well in the exam.
   7   She is a brilliant student so, <u>of course</u>, we expect her to pass.
   8   She knew she would fail the exam <u>unless</u> she found a way to cheat.

—— 2 ——

a   1 apparently   2 generally   3 ideally
   4 eventually   5 luckily   6 hopefully
   7 originally   8 presumably   9 potentially

b   Here are some possible answers:
   1 . . . luckily I had a spare set in the house.
   2 . . . generally it's excellent.
   3 . . . eventually it should be a lot better.
   4 . . . ideally I'd like a new one.
   5 . . . apparently you have to pay.
   6 . . . originally it was just an ordinary little fishing port.

⋙→

7 . . . potentially it could be a great success.
8 . . . hopefully I'll pass this time.
9 . . . presumably she'll be here before you leave.

3

a Here are the appropriate general words:
1 material   2 facilities   3 expenses   4 crops   5 resources
6 pets   7 equipment   8 insects   9 weapons
10 belongings

4

b *measures, scheme,* and *proposal*: . . . underground roads linking major
routes into the capital, plus a programme of road improvements . . .
approach: . . . a number of open meetings . . .
issue: . . . the number of cars on our roads could double within 25 years.
(More generally it also refers back to the basic problem of traffic
congestion.)
rate: . . . double within twenty-five years . . .
aspects: . . . pollution levels . . . destruction of the Green Belt . . .
dilemma: . . . private motorists . . . environmental groups . . .

SELF-STUDY ACTIVITIES

2 despite = in spite of
considering that = in view of the fact that
in addition = moreover

but = however
as long as = provided
needless to say = of course

17 **Technology:** Teacher's notes

—— 1 ——

a Students can work on the activity individually and then compare their answers. Allow them to use dictionaries to help them. The focus of the exercise is on the vocabulary of definitions rather than the objects themselves, so when you check the answers clarify the meaning and use of words such as *device, instrument, system, branch* and so on. *Device* and *instrument* are quite difficult to separate, they can be interchangeable sometimes, but *instrument* is often preferred when the object performs a task requiring great precision, e.g. measuring something. *Device* can cover a range of objects which would include *instruments* and *gadgets*, e.g. a pilot has an *instrument panel*; a doctor uses *surgical instruments*; a kitchen may contain various *devices* to help in the preparation of food; a tyre-pressure gauge may conceivably be described as an *instrument* or a *device*.

b Students can now complete this activity individually or in pairs. Check the answers and then let them work on **c** individually or in pairs.

—— 2 ——

a Tell the students to write down anything they think is a possible answer, and move round the groups and help them with vocabulary they may need to describe the different gadgets.

b This exchange of information will help the groups to build a longer list of possible answers, and to resolve certain vocabulary problems they may be having. Discuss the answers with the class without confirming or rejecting any suggestions.

c Divide the class in half so that some groups read the first set of texts while other groups go on to the set of texts on p. 124. Move round and help students where necessary. When they have finished, you can put the groups together again to discuss the answers. In this activity students will be actively teaching words that they discovered in their texts to students who haven't seen the text. At the end, groups can read the remaining texts.

In this type of exercise students can learn a lot of new vocabulary, but each student is likely to focus on different things and so by the end of the exercise you may not be sure who has learnt what. This should not worry you provided the students have been actively engaged in the different parts of the exercise, but if you wish to draw the vocabulary together at the end, you could ask the students to tell each other what they have learnt, and then conduct a short feedback with the group in which you put key words on the board, e.g. *inaccurate, battery operated, neat, relieve pain, stainless steel, insert, attach, stapler, hygienic, amplifier, blood pressure, portable* and so on.

—— 3 ——

a Make sure your students understand the words in the list.

b Play the tape and give the students time to write their answers, i.e. stop the tape after each dialogue for about thirty seconds. At the end, students can compare their answers in pairs before you discuss them with the class. Explain new words as necessary.

c This provides the students with an added reason to listen to the tape a second time and makes them think about the range of application / use of certain words and phrases, e.g. *dirt* and *dust*.

d Tell the students to read through the questionnaire first to see if they understand the vocabulary. Explain any new items briefly, e.g. *fiddle, puncture, tune in, leak*. Then put them into groups to discuss their answers.

—— 4 ——

a This is a fun activity, although it does provide students with an idea they can use for their own vocabulary storage (see **3** in the *Self-study activities*). Play the tape to exemplify the words in their book, and play it a second time if necessary.

b Omit this activity if you have an adult group who may find this activity silly or childish; some groups love it.

c Building associations between sounds and the situations in which they occur is often a very effective way for students to remember these words.

SELF-STUDY ACTIVITIES

2 If your students are studying in an English speaking country, they may be able to bring in a gadget/instrument belonging to the host family they are staying with (if they are staying with a family). If not, try and take in some gadgets/instruments of your own.

3 Most students keep a notebook for vocabulary records, but a cassette library can be very motivating and extremely practical: learners can listen to their recordings while they are in the car. And, of course, a cassette library does ensure there is far greater attention given to pronunciation.

The hardest part is getting your students to make a start on their library, so it may be a good idea to do some recordings in class. If you have access to several cassette recorders, divide the class into groups (preferably in different rooms), and ask them to do this exercise. They can then listen to the efforts of each group in turn, try and identify each of the sounds as they listen, and vote on the best recording for each sound. It can be great fun.

17 Technology:
Key words and expressions

Nouns		Verbs	Adjectives
alternative	stapler	absorb	damp
amplifier	telescope	attach	(in)accurate
battery	thermometer	bang	ingenious
device		buzz	neat
dirt		fiddle	portable
dust		flicker	
electric drill		gurgle	
instrument		hiss	
knob		leak	
lead		magnify	
lever		measure	
photocopier		relieve (pain)	
plug		screech	
plumber		squeak	
printer		tick	
radiator		treat (an illness)	
speedometer		tune (sth.) in	

Other words and expressions

background noise
branch, e.g. of medicine
faulty connection
go and look for sth. or sb.
hard of hearing

have a look at sth.
press a button
stainless steel
try and fix sth.
try and work it out (for oneself)

SELF-STUDY ACTIVITIES

auto-focus or zoom lens
brand new or second hand (car)
digital or analogue clock
hard or floppy disc
laser or dot matrix printer

mains or portable (radio)
manual or automatic gearbox
record or tape deck

bark
growl
howl
mumble
tap

17 **Technology:** Key

───── **1** ─────────────────────────

a 1 telex   2 barometer   3 thermostat   4 microscope
5 radiology   6 physiotherapy

b 1 An *instrument* for *measuring* . . .   thermometer
2 A *device* that . . .   microphone
3 The *treatment* of illness *using* . . .   psychotherapy
4 A *device* for *sending* . . .   telephone
5 An *instrument* . . .   telescope
6 A *branch* of *science* which *involves* . . .   thermodynamics

c Here are possible definitions:
  1 A microwave is a device for heating food and drink involving the use of microwaves.
  2 A speedometer is an instrument for measuring the speed of a vehicle.
  3 A radio is a device for sending or receiving sound over long distances by the use of radio waves.

───── **2** ─────────────────────────

c 1 A sound way to relieve pain.
  2 One touch monitors your blood pressure
  3 The staple-less stapler
  4 The ashtray that actually freshens the air
  5 The portable telephone amplifier
  6 Under pressure?
  7 The first cordless travel iron
  8 Remove unwanted hair hygienically

© Cambridge University Press 1991

─── **3** ───────────────────────────

b 🖭

Object	How do you know?
1 television	interference, flickering, I can't get a proper picture
2 electric drill	I've only made a couple of holes in the wall
3 washing machine	cycle, when I take things out they're still damp
4 camera	to wind on, automatic when you take a picture
5 photocopier	paper's getting jammed, they're not coming through, take a look inside
6 typewriter	keys keep sticking; why not buy electronic one

c Other words relevant to problems with machines and appliances are:
  1 It keeps flickering . . . (common problem with televisions)
  2 . . . faulty connection. (common with electrical appliances)
      . . . dust or dirt has got into it. (common with machines in general)
  3 There's definitely something wrong with it . . . (you know there's a
      problem but don't know what it is)
      . . . it's leaking . . . (common for any machine using water)
  4 Is the battery OK? (common problem with cameras, watches, cars,
      torches, Walkmans, certain kinds of toy, etc.)
  5 . . . there's a burning smell . . . (problem often associated with
      electrical goods)

─────── | **SELF-STUDY ACTIVITIES** | ───────

1 Here are possible answers:
   a) car / bicycle   e) clock / watch
   b) lens   f) deck
   c) disc   g) recorder / radio
   d) printer   h) gearbox / car

© Cambridge University Press 1991

18 Revision and expansion:
Teacher's notes

1

Textual synonymy is a very common feature of discourse, and awareness of this fact can often help students to guess the meaning of unknown words in a text. (Further examples of exercises which exploit textual synonymy and antonymy can be found in *A Way with Words 1* and *2*.)

2

You can extend this activity by asking students to try and find more compound words using at least one word from the compound, for example:

spare room / spare wheel	pay rise / sunrise
status symbol / sex symbol	stock market / black market
pulse rate / interest rate	air fares / bus fares

3

Follow the instructions in the Student Book.

4

Follow the instructions in the Student Book.

5

Pronunciation exercises are an excellent way to recycle vocabulary, and the frequency of the schwa / ə / in English means that you can reproduce exercises of this type for a wide range of lexical items; it is especially useful for word building activities as many suffixes contain this sound, e.g. -able, -ness, -ment and -ous.

6

When the students have completed the article they can look back over the similar texts in Unit 13.

—— **7** ————————————————————————

This activity can produce lively and amusing conversations with some students and dull meaningless repetitions with others; it depends on their mood at the time. If it works well, you can extend it by feeding in new verbs, written on bits of paper, while the students are talking. This is a wise strategy to prompt a shift in the conversation if you sense it is becoming repetitive.

—— **8** ————————————————————————

Put the students in pairs or groups and encourage them to think of different possible answers for each sentence and to be as specific as possible, e.g. the answers to 1 might include a basement room, a prison cell, their classroom and a tent. Sentence 2 could be a filling, an injection, an examination, etc.

—— **9** ————————————————————————

This can be done orally although it is advisable to give the students one or two minutes to think about their answers, otherwise the activity loses its momentum and suffers from too many pauses and hesitations.

—— **10** ————————————————————————

Tell the students that the length of their sentences need not be governed by the length of the gap in the book; their answers can be as short or as long as they wish, but they must provide an appropriate syntactic pattern for each verb. They can discuss their sentences with a partner before you check the answers with the whole class.

—— **11** ————————————————————————

The activity revises and consolidates a number of superordinates, e.g. *facilities* and *insects*, but the actual answers may unearth all sorts of new items, so let students use dictionaries, and be prepared to move round the groups and help them if they are searching for a particular word or phrase.

—— **12** ————————————————————————

This is another activity using pronunciation to recycle a wide range of lexical items, and is also an activity that can work well or badly depending on the mood of the group and/or the students' personalities. If it works well, you can repeat it on other occasions by changing the sound each time.

18 Revision and expansion:
New words and expressions

bat
draughty
lap
van
vibration
waterproof

18   Revision and expansion: Key

1

---

1 transmit   2 relieves   3 taking a short cut   4 portable
5 rather   6 tabloids   7 surrendered   8 explosion   9 turn up
10 attach

2

---

dishwasher   stainless steel   fitted carpet   painkiller
spare room   trade union   air fares   status symbol   pay rise
background noise   stock market   public opinion   pulse rate
weather forecast   vacuum cleaner   food mixer

3

Here are some possible answers:
alcove   armchair   ashtray   balcony   coffee table   cupboard
curtains   fireplace   French window   garden   hedge   mirror
patio   picture   rug   shelves   sofa   television   vase

4

---

1 in spite of/despite
2 although
3 in view of the fact/considering
4 in view of
5 unless
6 provided (that)/as long as
7 in case
8 However
9 of course/however/needless to say
10 Moreover/In addition

© Cambridge University Press 1991

104

5

ambulance   psychology   necessary   instrument

corruption   emergency   interested   thermometer

presumably   microphone   document   potentially

paragraph   alternative   temperature   machinery

6

Here are some possible answers:

para. 1: threatened/promised
       rise/claim
para. 2: spokesman/spokeswoman
para. 3: unions

para. 4: dispute
       negotiation
para. 5: warned/said
para. 6: leaders/negotiators
       promised/pledged
       emergency

8

Here are some possible answers:
1 a cellar / room / flat
2 an injection / filling
3 a desk / garden
4 travelling iron / computer / a gadget
5 a watch
6 a car / bike / gate
7 a television / video
8 a knife / tin
9 wine
10 a tent

9

1 A thermometer is an instrument for measuring temperature.
2 A stapler is a device for fixing pieces of paper together.
3 A microscope is an instrument which magnifies very small objects.
4 A stock market is the place where you can buy and sell shares.
5 A loft is a space below the roof of a house which can be used for storage.
6 A basement is a room or rooms in a house below street level.

≫→

7 A telescope is an instrument which makes distant objects appear larger and nearer.
8 A microphone is a device that you speak into to record or amplify your voice.
9 A wardrobe is a piece of furniture in the bedroom where you hang clothes.

—— 10 ——

Here are some possible answers:
1 He agreed *to help me with my* homework.
2 She encouraged *me to spend* the money.
3 He let *me use* his car.
4 I'm thinking *of going to Greece for my* holiday.
5 She suggested *that I have dinner* with them.
6 I regret *leaving school* at sixteen.
7 He insisted *that he pay for the* meal.
8 I'm used *to getting up at seven* o'clock.
9 I don't remember *putting it on my* desk.
10 I'm looking forward *to going there in the* spring.

—— 11 ——

a   Here are some possible answers:
1 air-conditioning / a fax machine / a mini bar in your room
2 cockroaches / mosquitos / giant spiders
3 a wheel-brace (spanners) / a jack
4 a good tent / a sleeping bag / a gas stove
5 a stethoscope / scales / a syringe / a blood pressure gauge
6 rice / soya beans
7 watches / drugs / alcohol / cigarettes

19 **Customs:** Teacher's notes

--- **1** ---

a Most students are fascinated by cross-cultural differences, but whenever they talk about it they often resort to a very restricted range of vocabulary, for example, 'In my country it is usual / very bad to . . .' The focus of this exercise is a wider range of expressions to talk about this subject, for example, 'In Spain it is customary / considered bad manners to . . .'

Put the students in groups and ask them to discuss the ten statements. Conduct a feedback session to find out their answers but without saying if they are right or wrong; their desire to know the correct answers provides the motivation for the listening.

b 🔲 Tell the students to write down the correct answers as they listen. The passage is quite long and, if possible, we would recommend that you record it in the language laboratory so your students can listen individually at their own pace. If this facility is not available, you could play it in the classroom in two sections. When you have checked the answers you can put the students in groups for **1c**. Clearly this activity will be more interesting for a mixed nationality class, although it is surprising how often students from the same country disagree about their own cultural behaviour.

--- **2** ---

a We normally ask students to complete **2a** and **2b** at the same time, and we put students in pairs or small groups and ensure that each pair/group has access to a bilingual and monolingual dictionary. If you work in a country where the students may have difficulty with some of the concepts for cultural reasons, e.g. not all wedding ceremonies will have a best man, ask the students to complete as much as they can, and then explain these concepts at the end.

c With a single nationality group this quiz provides vocabulary practice; with a mixed nationality group it often sparks off a lot of discussion which can create a need for more lexical input.

─── **3** ───────────────────────

a The students will be able to complete the grid with the aid of the pictures and dictionaries, but before you put them into groups to discuss their answers you should check the pronunciation of *prawns* / prɔːnz /, *cucumber* / kjuːkʌmbə /, and *cabbage* / kæbɪdʒ /.

b Follow the instructions in the Student Book and allow the use of dictionaries for students to find the meanings of new words, e.g. *tender* and *sieve*. Discuss the answers with the class when they have finished.

A further practice activity would be for the students to write down the ingredients and cooking method for a dish with which they are familiar. This is best done in pairs or groups as some students may know very little about cooking.

──────┤ **SELF-STUDY ACTIVITIES** ├──────────

1 If you ask your students to do this exercise at home, you could walk into the next lesson and provide the stimuli which may prompt them to reply with some of the phrases, for example:

It's my birthday today.

I've just passed an exam.

'Sneeze'.

The students can go on to discuss some of the other words and phrases in groups.

2 Follow the instructions in the Student Book. If your students know each other well, you could discuss the likelihood of each person keeping to their resolutions.

3 With a mixed nationality group this can lead to an interesting discussion on festivals and holidays in different countries.

19 Customs:
Key words and expressions

Weddings	Funerals	Cooking	Food
aisle	ashes	bake	cabbage
best man	burial/to bury	boil	celery
bouquet	cemetery	brown (v)	crab
bride	coffin	chop	cucumber
bridesmaid	cremation	eat raw	egg yolks
ceremony	(funeral) service	flour	garlic
groom/bridegroom	grave	frying pan	kidney
honeymoon	undertaker	fry/sauté	liver
reception	wreath	grill	mussels
registry office		mince	parsley
priest/vicar		sieve	peppers
		simmer	shrimps/prawns
		steam	squid
		stir	tripe
		stock	
		strain	

Other words and expressions

attract sb.'s attention
blow one's nose
customary
fairly common
it is considered { rude to . . .
{ bad manners to . . .

rare
shake hands
social greeting
surname
tend to . . .
to address someone

SELF-STUDY ACTIVITIES

bless you
cheers
congratulations
cut down (on sth.)

good luck
hear hear!
I beg your pardon

many happy returns
once upon a time
say cheese

© Cambridge University Press 1991

19 Customs: Key

——— 1 ———————————————————

b 🔲

1 true   2 false   3 true   4 false   5 false   6 false
7 true   8 (usually) false   9 impossible to generalize   10 false

——— 2 ———————————————————

a *Weddings*: bride   ceremony   church   ring   reception
aisle   groom   vicar/priest   bridesmaid   honeymoon
service   best man   registry office   bouquet
Funerals: church   burial   undertaker   aisle   ashes
vicar/priest   coffin   cemetery   cremation   grave   wreath
service

b

People	Events	Places	Things
bride	cremation	cemetery	wreath
groom	service	church	ring
vicar/priest	ceremony	grave	bouquet
undertaker	reception	registry office	coffin
bridesmaid	honeymoon	aisle	ashes
best man	burial		

c Most answers will depend on the nationality / religion of the students, but the answer to question 6 is London, and the answer to 7 is Dracula.

——— 3 ———————————————————

b 1 Brazil   2 China   3 Spain   4 Greece

© Cambridge University Press 1991

SELF-STUDY ACTIVITIES

1 *Once upon a time*: traditionally used at the beginning of children's stories
  cheers: something people say to each other just before they have an
    alcoholic drink
  bless you: what you say when someone sneezes
  say cheese: something that you say to make someone smile when you take
    their photograph
  good luck: a way of saying that you hope someone will be successful in
    something
  congratulations: something you say when someone has done well in
    something, e.g. passed an exam
  I beg your pardon: a way of saying 'sorry', e.g. you step on someone's foot
  I beg your pardon?: a way of asking someone to repeat something
  hear hear!: a way of agreeing with what someone has said (formal)
  many happy returns: is what you say to someone on their birthday

2 Here are some possible answers:
  a) I'm going to give up smoking.
  b) I'm going to cut down on chocolate.
  c) I'm going to be more punctual.
  d) I'm going to spend more time with my family.
  e) I'm going to stop being bad tempered in the mornings.
  f) I'm going to remember to write to my pen friend every week.
  g) I'm going to improve my English.
  h) I'm going to get more exercise.

3 14 February is Valentine's Day.
  1 April is April Fool's Day.
  The Friday before Easter is called Good Friday.
  31 October is Halloween (this is more important in the United States than
  Great Britain).
  5 November is Bonfire/Guy Fawkes Night.
  24 December is Christmas Eve.
  25 December is Christmas Day.
  26 December is Boxing Day.
  31 December is New Year's Eve.

20 **Multi-word units:** Teacher's notes

1

There is no single correct strategy for learning words from a text, but if students do employ strategies for learning and pursue them conscientiously, they are more likely to learn than students who have no strategy for dealing with new words in a text. This exercise is primarily a consciousness raising activity, but also encourages students to experiment with new strategies.

a When the students have finished the reading activity they can compare their answers in groups. It is normally the case that some students will have asked you to explain certain words in the text rather than employ one of the strategies mentioned. This provides an ideal starting point to discuss **1b**, and may also raise the issue of your own role in the classroom: are you there to provide answers or to develop the students' ability to learn for themselves?

c This activity has a clearer focus if each student names the strategy they are going to use. When they have finished, students can talk to others who used the same strategy and then to students who used a different one. At the end you can discuss the conclusions with the whole group.

2

a Students can do this individually or in pairs. When they have finished they should move on to **2b**. Check the answers at the end of this second activity. (If you go through the questions after **2a** you will almost certainly give away many of the answers to **2b**.)

c Check the answers before the students practise the dialogues in pairs.

d Make sure the students are aware of the position of a pronoun used with a separable phrasal verb, e.g. pick it up, and *not* 'pick up it'.

3

a Follow the instructions in the Student Book.

b This can sometimes produce very amusing answers. Tell the students that if their complete sentences do not make sense, they should amend them so that they do.

4

a Put the students in pairs and allow them to use dictionaries to help them find the meaning of the phrasal verbs and idiomatic expressions in the box. It may be advisable for the students to write their answers initially, and then you can check them with the class before moving on to **4b**.

The controlled practice can be made more interesting if you ask the students to add something to each of their replies, for example:

1 A: D'you want me to wait?
   B: Yes, could you hang on a minute? I've got to speak to my brother for a minute.
2 A: I find her very irritating, don't you?
   B: Yes, she really gets on my nerves; she never stops talking.

SELF-STUDY ACTIVITIES

1 The students should be able to complete this activity with the aid of dictionaries, but you may wish to check their answers in a future lesson.

2 Common collocations are sometimes found in the sentence examples accompanying a dictionary definition, but this is not always the case so you may need to go through the exercise in class. Students can practise the collocations by thinking of a stimulus which will elicit one of the collocations as a suitable reply, for example:

A: Was it well organized?
B: No, it was utter chaos.

A: Do you feel OK?
B: No, I've got a splitting headache.

3 You could ask the students to exchange examples of their stories in class; this may help to get students into the habit of using this simple but effective revision strategy.

20 Multi-word units:
Key words and expressions

Phrasal verbs

get through (= make contact)
get through (= pass an exam)
get by (= manage)
get over sth. (= recover)
give up (= sacrifice)
give up (= stop doing)
go off (= explode)
go off sth. (= stop liking)
hold sb. up (= delay)
hold sth. up (= support)
pick sth./sb. up (= collect)
put sth. off (= postpone)
put sth. out (= extinguish)
see sb. off (= say goodbye)
set off (= begin a journey)
sort sth. out (= organize)
split up (= separate)
trip over (= fall)
try sth. on (= put on in a shop)
try sth. out (= test sth. to judge
   usefulness)
turn sth. down (= reduce volume)
turn sth. down (= reject)
turn sth. up (= increase volume)
turn up (= arrive)
work sth. out (= deduce / calculate)

Phrases

be in touch
get a move on
get hold of sb.
get on one's nerves
get rid of sth.
give sb. a lift
hang on
in the end
keep an eye on sth./sb.
off the beaten track
pick up a bug (= catch a virus)
pour with rain
take it in turns
tear something to pieces

Other words and expressions

appalling   excursion
cough   get soaked
cushion   limp
develop (a film)   lousy
dreadful   upset

SELF-STUDY ACTIVITIES

all alone	fast asleep	splitting headache
at a guess	for a change	thick fog
bone idle	for good	utter chaos
bored stiff	in return	vast majority
by return of post	narrow escape	wide range
by sight	off-hand	without fail
dire trouble	sheer coincidence	

© Cambridge University Press 1991

20 Multi-word units: Key

a 1 c   2 h   3 f   4 l   5 g   6 a   7 i   8 d   9 k
10 b   11 e   12 j

b Here are some possible answers:

1 an item of clothing	7 a mess in an office / room
2 a meeting	8 a mathematical problem
3 a cigarette	9 an illness
4 a word	10 smoking
5 a car / watch / jacket	11 a job
6 a machine of some sort	12 a radio / TV

c Here are some possible responses:

1 Yes, I'll put it out.
2 I don't know; look it up.
3 No, I've given it up.
4 Yes, but I turned it down.
5 Yes, could you turn it down a bit?
6 Can't you put it off?
7 Don't worry, I'll sort them out.
8 OK. Shall I pick it up tomorrow, then?
9 I couldn't work it out.
10 Yes, but she'll get over it.
11 Well, we won't know until we try it out.

d The other verbs are all separable; *get over* is inseparable.

── **3** ────────────────────────────

a   1 definition 2   2 definition 3   3 definition 4.2
   4 definition 5   5 definition 4.2   6 definition 2
   7 definition 2   8 definition 3

b   Possible answers are:

1 I lost it . . . I'll have to buy another one.
2 I asked him . . . China.
3 I tried to ring her . . . all the lines to Italy were busy.
4 She failed last time but if she . . . she works hard.
5 I set my alarm . . . been waiting long.
6 I used to drink a lot of wine . . . a headache.
7 I don't think that shelf is safe . . . you should do something about it.
8 I'm sorry I'm late . . . of a baggage handlers' strike.

c   The two meanings of *get through* are related, i.e. they both involve succeeding in something. The different meanings of the other verbs do not seem related, although some of the other dictionary meanings are connected, for example, *turn up* definitions 1 and 2 and *get through* definitions 1, 4, 5 and 6.

── **4** ────────────────────────────

a   Here are the correct verbs and phrases in possible answers:

1 Yeah, hang on.
2 Yes, she gets on my nerves.
3 Yes, it's a bit off the beaten track.
4 Yes, I can get by on that.
5 Yes, let's get rid of them.
6 Yes, they set off at 6 a.m.
7 Yes, they split up last year.
8 No, I couldn't get hold of him.
9 Yes, they tore it to pieces.
10 Yes, keep an eye on them, will you?
11 Yes, we take it in turns to use it.
12 Yes, get a move on.

© Cambridge University Press 1991

SELF-STUDY ACTIVITIES

1 a) I recognize him but I don't actually know him.
   b) I promise to give it to you tomorrow.
   c) Send it to me within a day of receiving it.
   d) There were approximately thirty of them.
   e) I don't know the answer at this moment, but I could probably find out
      for you.
   f) They've gone to America for ever, i.e. they are not coming back.
   g) First he gave me something and so I then gave him my cassettes.
   h) We don't go to the theatre very often.

2 vast majority   utter chaos   bone idle   narrow escape   bored stiff
   fast asleep   wide range   thick fog   all alone   sheer coincidence
   dire trouble   splitting headache

© Cambridge University Press 1991

21 Men and women: Teacher's notes

─── 1 ───────────────────────────

a Before the students complete the sentences, go through them and explain new words and phrases, e.g. *obsessed with*, *inclined to*, and so on. In many cases, the target word or phrase in each sentence will be familiar to the students, but rarely a part of the student's active vocabulary, e.g. *tend to*, *unlike*, *one thing that X and Y have in common*. In other cases, the vocabulary is a common source of error, e.g. *on the other hand*, *compared with*. The focus of the exercise, therefore, is practice rather than lengthy presentation.

b When the students have completed the sentences – you can try to discourage facetious or stereotyped examples – the students can compare and discuss their answers.

c The cartoon does present a lighthearted view of the male brain, so in this activity you should expect some fairly jocular stereotyping. If you wish to avoid this, omit the activity.

─── 2 ───────────────────────────

a Tell the students to read through the questions and use dictionaries to help them with new words; explain new items yourself where necessary.

b ▭ Explain the rubric in the Student Book and then play the cassette, pausing after each reply so that the students have time to look through the questions and put their answers in. Check the answers at the end and highlight key words and phrases from the cassette on the board, e.g. *used to doing sth.*, *child minder*, use of *object* as a verb, *sacrifice*, *work under pressure*, and so on.

c Follow the instructions in the Student Book. With adult groups you could find out if any members of the class have been asked any of these questions at job interviews.

——— **3** ———————————————————————————

a While the students are working on this activity, move round the class and help them with the meanings of difficult items. If you anticipate that some items will be new for the whole group, you may decide to pre-teach them before setting the task.

b Follow the instructions in the Student Book.

c It is important to stress that the word chains may consist of four words or fourteen words, and that there is no correct answer; students simply build associations which reflect their own views, attitudes and experience. We have found this type of activity to be a very memorable learning process for some students, while others have a very lukewarm response. This is inevitable because people learn in different ways, but if you are worried by this potential conflict you could offer an alternative activity in which the students have to subdivide the list into positive, neutral and negative words.

d You could omit this activity if you are short of time, or give it for homework.

——— **4** ———————————————————————————

a Put the students in pairs or groups and make sure they have access to dictionaries – they will not be able to complete this activity without them.

b When they have finished, they can join with another pair/group and discuss the answers.

——— | **SELF-STUDY ACTIVITIES** | ————————————————

1 The students will be able to find the answers in a bilingual dictionary or a good monolingual dictionary as common opposites are often cross-referenced in the dictionary entry, e.g. in the entry for *nephew* in the Longman Dictionary of Contemporary English it states – compare NIECE.

2 Students can compare their answers in a future lesson.

21 Men and women:
Key words and expressions

Nouns		Verbs	Adjectives
anger	hypocrisy	blush	aware (of)
betrayal	lads	cope (with)	bushy
birth	mood	dig	defiant
brooch	oppression	envy	fierce
butcher	poetry	fold	irritating
child minder	poverty	giggle	loyal
compassion	rape	glance (at)	obsessed (with)
comradeship	riot	object (to sth.)	slender
dressing gown	sensitivity	pace (up and down)	tanned
doorstep	sleeve	show off	temporary
envy	slippers	slouch	weather-beaten
eyebrow	suffering	stroll	willing
flattery	sweat	sweep	wrinkled
gang	tights	tease	
hips	tune	whistle	

Other words and expressions

compared with X, Y . . .
does X mind Y -ing . . .?
how do you feel about -ing. . .?
I can't resist the temptation
inclined to . . .
in my experience . . .
likely to . . .
make a commitment

members of the opposite sex
one thing X and Y have in common is that. . .
on the other hand
start a family
under pressure
unlike X, Y . . .
take (time) off
what do you do for a living?

SELF-STUDY ACTIVITIES
---

actor / actress
bridegroom / bride
bull / cow
cock / hen
headmaster / headmistress

hero / heroine
host / hostess
landlord / landlady
masculine / feminine
monastery / convent

monk / nun
nephew / niece
waiter / waitress
widower / widow

21   Men and women: Key

─── **1** ───────────────────────

Here are some possible answers:
1 In my experience men are (much) more egotistical than women.
2 Women, on the other hand, tend to be more sensitive than men.
3 Men are often obsessed with football.
4 Women are more inclined to be aware of other people's feelings than men.
5 Unlike men, women's voices don't break.
6 The most irritating thing about men is that they forget birthdays and anniversaries.
   The most irritating thing about women is that they remember birthdays and anniversaries.
7 Compared with men, women are less hairy.
   Compared with women, men are more muscular.
8 One thing that men and women both have in common is that they need each other.

─── **2** ───────────────────────

b 📼 1 L   2 A   3 G   4 D   5 E   6 J   7 H   8 B
    9 K   10 C   11 F   12 I

─── **4** ───────────────────────

a Here are possible answers:
   1 She   2 he   3 He   4 She she   5 He his   6 him
   7 girls   8 he his   9 He/she his/her her   10 his he his
   11 she   12 He he he   13 She her her
   14 he/she his/her   15 She

SELF-STUDY ACTIVITIES

1 a) masculine
   b) niece
   c) actress
   d) bridegroom
   e) hostess
   f) widow
   g) waitress
   h) nun
   i) monastery
   j) headmistress
   k) bull
   l) cock
   m) heroine
   n) landlord

22 Ways of saying things:
Teacher's notes

—— 1 ——

a It is extremely difficult to make categorical statements about the appropriateness of language in different situations, although students often crave for definitive right or wrong answers. At the risk of becoming over simplistic we have found that the exercise is more successful if the students relate each of the requests to the criteria at the top of the page; this seems to satisfy their desire for a 'concrete' task. They can work on the activity individually or in pairs.

b Follow the instructions in the Student Book, check the answers at the end and clarify the meaning of any new words and phrases.

c You could do this as a class activity.

d This activity is more fun if the students move freely round the class asking different people different questions. It can also be made more authentic with a few minor changes to the situations, for example:
one student could ask another for help in moving their desk;
one student could ask you if they could miss the next lesson;
one student could ask another group of students to keep the noise down a bit;
one student could ask another group if they minded having the window open;
and so on.

—— 2 ——

a/b When the students have had a go at **2a** they can listen to the tape to check their answers and/or to learn new vocabulary items.

c This can be omitted if you are short of time.

—— 3 ——

a You can follow the instructions in the Student Book, but if you wish to make the activity more concrete, you could assign roles. For example, tell one student that he or she works for a right-wing newspaper and tell another that he or she works for a left-wing one. For the second passage, one student should convey a positive attitude and the other a negative attitude.

d After the students have compared their answers you can clarify any problems. As a follow-up, you could bring a newspaper article to class – preferably on a controversial topic – and see if the students can change the tone of the article by adding or replacing a few words and phrases.

—— **4** ————————————————————————————

a The impact of the poem may be lost on students who are more worried about looking up the new vocabulary. If you sense that may happen with your group, pre-teach the new items first (e.g. *bully, sneaky, gabble, hug, fizzy*) and then read the poem to them slowly. If necessary, read the poem twice, and then ask them to tell you the things that the poet dislikes about words. When you have a list on the board, you can let the students read the poem and they can then add anything to the list they missed.

b It may help to give an example: *Words give the poet a fright, but words can also comfort people.*

c The sentences in the book are quite impersonal, but it is much more fun if you replace the pronouns with the names of students in the class, e.g. *Although it was quite shallow, Marcel sank like . . .*

—— **SELF-STUDY ACTIVITIES** ————————————————

1 Traditionally, similes are formed with *as . . . as . . .* but with fixed idiomatic similes the first *as* is often deleted. You can check the answers in a future lesson.

2 For further practice in class, you could ask the students to rank the sayings in different ways. For example, which ones express the greatest truth? Which ones are the most useful?

3 Students can compare their answers in groups in a future lesson.

22 Ways of saying things:
Key words and expressions

Nouns	Verbs	Adjectives
bully	arrest	broke (inf.)
demonstrator	charge	cosy
disturbance	flare up	cramped
ditch	float	facial
drag (inf.)	gabble	fizzy
hug	hug	mean
kids (inf.)	pinch (inf.)	nasty
know-how (inf.)	reckon (inf.)	overgrown
quid (inf.)	retaliate	packed
riot shield	scream	rowdy
stick	shove	starving (inf.)
stream	squeak	thriving
thug	yell	tied up
troublemaker		thick (inf.)
wound		unbearable
		(un)spoilt

Other words and expressions

a running battle
could you spare me a minute?
do you fancy . . .? (inf.)
do you happen to know . . .?
do you mind if I . . .?
do you think I/you could possibly . . .?
give someone a hand
have a word with someone
I bet (= I'm sure) (inf.)
I haven't the faintest idea
I was wondering if . . .?

in need of
in the middle of nowhere
keep the noise down
loads of (time) (inf.)
once you get the hang of it (inf.)
on top of that
to make matters worse
what's up? (inf.)
within easy reach of
would you rather I didn't . . .?

SELF-STUDY ACTIVITIES

blind as a bat	A bad workman always blames his tools.
cunning as a fox	Actions speak louder than words.
dry as a bone	Familiarity breeds contempt.
deaf as a post	Let sleeping dogs lie.
good as gold	Make a mountain out of a molehill.
light as a feather	Practice makes perfect.
red as a beetroot	The grass is always greener on the other side.
selling like hot cakes	Two wrongs don't make a right.
sleep like a log	
white as a sheet	
bet	
drag	
handy	
load	
pinch	
starve	

22 **Ways of saying things:** Key

1
---

a 1 a   2 b   3 a   4 b   5 a   6 b   7 b   8 b

b Here are some possible answers:
1b would be correct talking to a stranger in a hotel or public building.
2a would be correct with a friend.
3b would be correct talking to a colleague rather than close friend.
4a would be correct with a friend.
5b would be correct with someone you didn't know (or perhaps a close friend if you thought you might receive a negative answer).
6a would be correct with a friend.
7a would be correct with someone you knew well (or with a stranger as long as you were certain to receive a positive answer).
8a would be correct with someone you know well (or with a stranger as long as you were certain to receive a positive answer).

c 1 2a   5 8b
2 4b   6 3a or 3b
3 6a or 6b   7 5a or 5b
4 1a   8 7a or 7b

2
---

b 1 loads   2 starving   3 handy   4 kids
5 once you get the hang of it   6 pinched   7 a real drag   8 I bet
9 up   10 know-how   11 reckon   12 d'you fancy a bite to eat

——— 3 ———

a Here are two possible interpretations for each text:
1 a Trouble . . . flared up . . . gang . . . rowdy . . . thugs . . .
      charged . . . defended themselves . . . riot shields . . . a running
      battle . . . leading troublemakers . . . a number of . . . nasty head
      wounds.
   b Problems . . . started . . . group . . . noisy . . . demonstrators . . .
      pushed towards . . . retaliated . . . sticks . . . quite a disturbance . . .
      demonstrators . . . several . . . facial injuries.
2 a . . . cosy . . . with many original features . . . unspoilt . . . small
      stream . . . What's more . . . a quiet peaceful setting / but / within
      easy reach of . . . now attracts a number of overseas visitors . . .
      a busy, thriving centre.
   b . . . cramped . . . badly in need of modernization . . .
      overgrown . . . smelly ditch . . . To make matters worse . . . in the
      middle of nowhere / and / miles from . . . is now packed with
      foreign tourists . . . almost unbearable.

——— 4 ———

a Words give him a fright   words are bullies
    sneaky things   They gabble and lie
    trying to understand them makes me cry   words hurt
    they get shoved in my face   words are mean
    words spread nasty gossip
    they lock me away from what I want to say   they make me sick

c Here are possible answers:

1 a duck / a lifebuoy	6	old cheese
2 a stone / a brick	7	a hyena / a parrot
3 a mouse	8	poetry
4 a blanket / a tablecloth	9	animals
5 a horse / a pig	10	a battlefield

SELF-STUDY ACTIVITIES

1 a) sheet   b) post   c) bat   d) log   e) feather   f) gold
  g) beetroot h) hot cakes   i) bone   j) fox

2 a) What you do is more important than what you say.
  b) To make a big fuss about something quite trivial.
  c) Don't create problems, leave things as they are.
  d) People often look for someone/something to blame rather than
     acknowledge their own mistakes.
  e) You only do something really well if you work at it.
  f) If you see someone too often you can take them for granted and even
     grow to despise them.
  g) Other people's situations always seem better than your own.
  h) If someone does something wrong to you, that is no justification for doing
     something wrong to them.

3 Here are some examples:
  Could you load those things on the lorry?
  Millions of people are starving in Africa.
  This tin-opener is a very handy gadget.
  That man pinched my arm.
  My suitcase was too heavy so I had to drag it along the floor.
  He bet me £5 I wouldn't be able to finish this exercise.

23 **Ideas and opinions:** Teacher's notes

1

a Follow the instructions in the Student Book. When the students have finished they can compare answers before you check them with the whole class.

b Rather than work from the book, write the five suggestions on the board – you can then change the suggestions and add your own if you feel they will be more relevant to your particular group.

c Seat the students in groups of five and explain the activity.

2

a As there are certain items in the text which will be new to most of the group, it may be quicker to pre-teach a few words and phrases, e.g. *access, toll, deter, lanes*. The students can then read the text and complete **2b**.

c When the students discuss their answers it is important that they do not simply read each other's sentences: tell them to take each scheme in turn and give each other their opinion of it using the phrases from **2b**. The meaning of the phrases being used in **2b** to express opinions should be quite transparent, but students do need practice in manipulating and activating this language, e.g. 'It sounds attractive but I doubt if it would work'.

3

a A number of vocabulary items in this exercise appeared in the previous exercise so the lexical load should not be too daunting. The students will probably need to use dictionaries to retrieve some of the answers, and you can check them before moving on to **3b**.

b This provides freer practice of some of the key items, and it is important the students do not look at the text during their discussion.

c When the students have read the text and you have checked the answers, you could exploit the text further by getting the students to produce a written reply. The reply could take the form of a letter of protest to a newspaper about the irresponsible and misleading nature of the article. The students could discuss their reply in groups and make notes, and then write the letter for homework.

d This final activity looks at the topic of addiction on a less serious and more personalized level, and you may wish to use it as a 'warmer' activity to start a future lesson.

SELF-STUDY ACTIVITIES

1 If the students have their own copies of the book, they can check their answers in the Word-building tables at the back.

2 Check the answers in a future lesson as a way of revising the different compound adjectives.

3 This is a further idea for vocabulary storage and you could ask the students to add more examples to the grid and then compare and discuss them in a future lesson.

23 Ideas and opinions:
Key words and expressions

Nouns	Verbs
abuse	abuse
access	amend
advertising / advertisement	assess
consumption / consumer	ban
deterrent	consume
fine	criticize
gadget	deter
imposition	(dis)agree (with sb./sth.)
jigsaw puzzle	double
knitting	drop (an idea/plan)
lane	evaluate
persuasion	go ahead (with sth.)
proposal	impose
reduction	put forward
restriction	reject
revenue	smuggle
ring road	warn
scheme	work (= be successful)
sewing	
smuggling	
(traffic) congestion	
warning	
workaholic	

Other words and expressions

(absolutely) ridiculous
DIY
elitist
I doubt if it'll work.
I'm (not) in favour of . . .
I'm (very much) against . . .
naive
in the long term
in practice
in theory

it sounds like a good idea
personally, I think . . .
season ticket
. . . sounds like a | good | idea
                    | great |
widespread
worldwide

SELF-STUDY ACTIVITIES

adaptation	hard-boiled	proposal
agreement	high-heeled	rejection
amendment	home-made	self-employed
assessment	law-abiding	short-sleeved / term
dismissal	long- term / sleeved	suggestion
evaluation	multi-national	time-consuming
far-fetched	narrow-minded	world-class

23 Ideas and opinions: Key

—— **1** ——

a 1 disagree with it   2 go ahead with it   3 evaluate it
4 drop it   5 carry on with it

b reject = dismiss   give up = drop
scheme = plan/idea   amend = adapt
put forward = propose/suggest   assess = evaluate

—— **3** ——

a

Verb	Noun(s)	Verb	Noun(s)
restrict	restriction	deter	deterrent
impose	imposition	abuse	abuse
advertise	advertising + advertisement	consume	consumer + consumption
produce	production + productivity	persuade	persuasion
reduce	reduction	tax	tax/taxation
warn	warning	smuggle	smuggling

c The text disagrees with all the statements in **2b**.

© Cambridge University Press 1991

SELF-STUDY ACTIVITIES

1

Verb	Noun	Verb	Noun
propose	proposal	assess	assessment
evaluate	evaluation	discuss	discussion
suggest	suggestion	reject	rejection
amend	amendment	adapt	adaptation + adaptor
dismiss	dismissal		
		agree	agreement

2 time-consuming job   world-class player   multi-national company
  long-term aim   law-abiding citizen   far-fetched story
  home-made cakes   self-employed builder   short-sleeved shirt
  hard-boiled egg   high-heeled shoes   narrow-minded attitude

24 Revision and expansion:
Teacher's notes

1

If you would like further practice of different verbs which describe ways of looking, walking, and so on, find a descriptive passage from a novel and rewrite it using more general verbs in place of the specific verb used (as in exercise **1**). You can then ask the students to try and provide more specific verbs which will give the passage more life and precision (you could also help them by giving them a box of words to choose from). This exercise not only practises these verbs in context but also acts as a reminder to students to try and use a range of vocabulary in their own writing; this is particularly useful for Cambridge exam students.

2

There are many answers which could be correct here so tell the students to move round and compare their dialogues and decide what is acceptable and what is not.

3

Follow the instructions in the Student Book.

4

Check the answers to **4a** before putting the students into groups for the discussion. This activity is more suitable for mixed nationality groups where there is a genuine interest in finding out what people do in different countries.

5

These examples come from units 19–23, but you could extend the activity by asking them to add further examples to each column from vocabulary in units 1–18.

—— **6** ————————————————————————————

Using one lexical set as a starting point to create different lexical sets, exploiting the different meanings of words or varied associations of words, can be a simple but effective way of expanding and consolidating different areas of vocabulary.

—— **7** ————————————————————————————

Follow the instructions in the Student Book.

—— **8** ————————————————————————————

Check the answers to **8a** before moving on to **8b**. The second activity is more fun if the students are able to think up amusing or unusual combinations in their sentences, and it may also help to make the activity (and the vocabulary) more memorable for the learners.

—— **9** ————————————————————————————

Follow the instructions in the Student Book.

—— **10** ————————————————————————————

a It is possible to use the same adjective for at least three of the sentences, e.g. *awful, dreadful, appalling* and *terrible* could all be used in sentences 4, 5, 6 and 8. In order to avoid this, tell the students that they must use a different adjective to respond to each sentence. Check the answers and then move on to **10b**.

For further practice you could put further degree adjectives on the board and then elicit appropriate extreme adjectives from the students, e.g. *big / enormous, cold / freezing, clever / brilliant*. In pairs, the students can then construct short dialogues around each pair of adjectives as in **10a**.

—— **11** ————————————————————————————

When the students have written their sentences, put them in pairs; one student reads out a sentence, and their partner has to produce another sentence using the target word with a different meaning.

12

Students can check their answers using the Word building tables at the back of the book.

13

You could ask the students to write their stories for homework but if you do make sure you will have sufficient examples of each story. In class, students who have written the same story can compare their answers first, and then they can regroup and compare their story with someone who wrote it from a different viewpoint.

14

When the students have completed the 'spider' diagram you could ask them, in pairs, to put each example into a sentence or to produce similar diagrams for other verbs, e.g. *make, do* or *take*.

15

Not all of these have clear opposites in terms of meaning, and so the students may produce a range of answers which they can discuss in pairs or groups.

16

With networks of this sort, I often ask students to complete it individually and then to think of ways of extending it with a partner. At the end, the pairs can compare their networks.

24 Revision and expansion:
New words and expressions

flood
naked

24 Revision and expansion: Key

Revision and expansion: Key

—— **1** —————————————————————————————

1 limping   2 strolling   3 pacing   4 glanced   5 staring
6 whispered   7 giggling   8 slouching

—— **2** —————————————————————————————

Here are some possible answers:
A: Do you happen to know where the post office is?
B: No, sorry, I haven't the faintest idea.

A: I was wondering if I could borrow your car?
B: Yeah, provided you drive carefully.

A: D'you fancy going to that new Italian restaurant?
B: Well actually, I'm not very keen on Italian food.

A: Would you mind if I opened the window?
B: No, go ahead.

A: D'you think I could possibly borrow your typewriter?
B: Yeah hang on, I'll go and get it for you.

—— **3** —————————————————————————————

a   think/reckon*   kids*/children   employ/take on*
tied up*/busy   manage/get by*   arrange/fix up*
delayed/held up*   know-how*/expertise   extinguish/put out*
get over*/recover

b   The words marked with an asterisk (*) are more informal.

—— **4** —————————————————————————————

a   1 Christmas Eve
2 Christmas Day
3 Boxing Day
4 New Year's Eve
5 New Year's Day

141

——— 5 ———

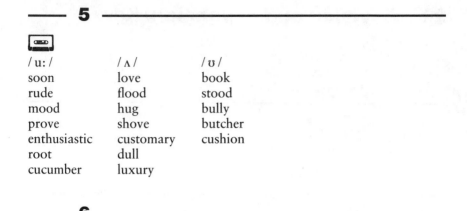

/ u: /	/ ʌ /	/ ʊ /
soon	love	book
rude	flood	stood
mood	hug	bully
prove	shove	butcher
enthusiastic	customary	cushion
root	dull	
cucumber	luxury	

——— 6 ———

Here are some possible answers:

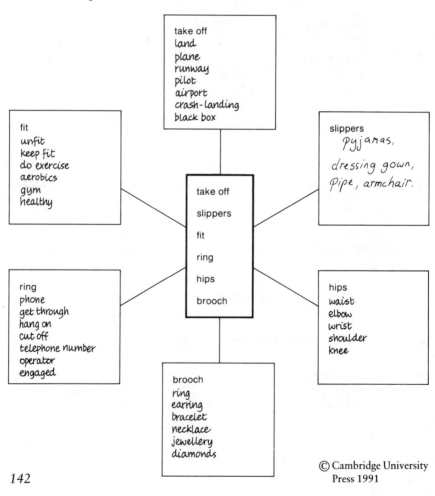

—— **8** ——————————————————————

whistle a tune   pour with rain   have a word   pay a fine
make sense   burst into flames   fold the paper   be in touch
shake hands   take time off   give someone a lift   blow one's nose
follow instructions   attract someone's attention

—— **9** ——————————————————————

[cassette] Words with one syllable:
suit   yacht   quite   reach   shocked   doubt   fares
suede   fuel   queue

Words with two syllables:
chaos   quiet   react   ruin   naked   poem   bias   riot
whereas   client

—— **10** ——————————————————————

Possible responses are:
1 Yes, I got absolutely soaked.
2 Yes, I'm absolutely starving.
3 Yes, absolutely ridiculous/stupid.
4 No, I feel absolutely lousy/awful/terrible.
5 Yes, absolutely awful/dreadful/terrible.
6 Yes, absolutely dreadful/appalling/awful/terrible.
7 Yeah, absolutely packed.
8 Yes, it was unbearable.

—— **11** ——————————————————————

Here are some possible answers:
I *gave up* smoking last year. (= stopped)
Would you *give up* your free time to work for nothing? (= sacrifice)

It's near the underground so it's very *handy* for work. (= convenient)
This is a very *handy* little dictionary. (= useful)

I *bet* you'll be pleased when this exam is over. (= I'm sure)
I never *bet* on races. (= gamble money)

I tried to phone but I couldn't *get through*. (= make contact)
I'm sure she'll *get through* the exam. (= pass)

》》》→

I'll *pick* you *up* at the hotel at seven. (= collect)
I *picked up* a virus when I was on holiday. (= contract an illness)
Could you *turn up* the radio? (= increase the volume)
He didn't *turn up* till gone ten. (= arrive)
I've still got *loads* of money. (= a lot)
They *loaded* the goods onto the lorry. (= put in)
My alarm clock didn't *go off* this morning. (= ring)
I was going to Spain, but I've *gone off* the idea now. (= lost interest)
Could you *turn down* the radio? (= reduce the volume)
I *turned down* her offer because I wanted more money. (= rejected)
We were *held up* for over an hour. (= delayed)
Just *hold up* your hands. (= raise)

--- **12** ---

1 poverty   2 assessment   3 criticism   4 deterrents
5 proposal   6 loyalty   7 consumption   8 anger

--- **14** ---

Here are some possible answers:

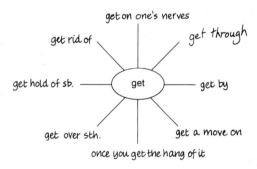

get on one's nerves
get rid of
get through
get hold of sb.
get
get by
get over sth.
get a move on
once you get the hang of it

— 15 —

Here are some possible answers:

upset ≠ pleased   tied up ≠ free   surname ≠ first name
nasty ≠ nice   cramped ≠ spacious   float ≠ sink
hypocrisy ≠ sincerity condemn ≠ condone off the beaten track ≠ near/
gold ≠ tin   yell ≠ whisper   convenient
birth ≠ death   spoilt ≠ unspoilt   fizzy ≠ flat/still
                                        feather ≠ brick

— 16 —

Here is a possible network:

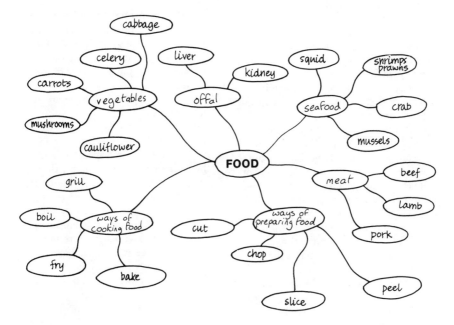

Tapescripts

Unit 3 Character and personality

Exercise 2d

Listen and follow the instructions in your book.

Man: I'm in most evenings and so I try to keep the place looking nice – not just because I like it to look nice but because I make an effort to get on with doing things at home and I find it much easier if the place is in some kind of order. It makes a big difference. I haven't got many things really; in fact I hate the idea of cluttering everything up with your possessions; it makes it so difficult if you ever want to move house, for a start. But having said that, I have got a colour TV and there's a piano – only an old second-hand one, but . . . but it works and, well, I'm not very good at it yet and don't suppose I ever will be but I've made up my mind to learn. Anyway, I make a point of practising at least half an hour every evening. I couldn't do without it really.
Apart from that well, there's the garden, which takes up quite a lot of my time, especially in the summer of course. I never knew very much about gardening before, but when I moved in here the previous owner had made quite a good job of it and I thought it would be a shame not to keep it going if I could.

Unit 4 Nouns

Exercise 2c

Listen and follow the instructions in your book.

Woman: Well, I was sitting in my next-door neighbour's kitchen and I looked out of the window and there was Fred.
Man: Fred.
Woman: My pet parrot. (Oh) Actually, his proper name is Frederick the Great, but he's usually just called Fred. Anyway, he was sitting on the branch of an apple tree at the bottom of the garden.
Man: Which is presumably where he's not meant to be.
Woman: Exactly. I mean I suppose I must have forgotten to close Fred's cage when I fed him earlier on, and then left a window open in the dining room. Anyway, Betty, my neighbour, dashed off to get her ladder from the cellar and I went outside to try and attract Fred's attention . . . and we got the ladder and we leant it carefully against the tree and I started to climb up. Fred meanwhile was watching all this with great interest . . . but when I got to the top of the ladder
Man: Don't tell me, he . . . he flew off.
Woman: Well not exactly. He started sort of fluttering about hysterically and then more or less fell onto the roof of the shed in the adjoining garden – the other side that is, not ours. Fortunately I was able to clamber down and crawl along the edge of the roof and when I was within about two feet of Fred I stuck my hand out and tried to grab hold of him – and I succeeded . . .

Man: Right.

Woman: Or at least I would've done if I hadn't overbalanced at that point.

Man: Oh oh oh.

Woman: I had to let go of him to try and get my balance back – failed, and ended up sliding off the roof and landing in a bed of roses below, which was very painful I might add.

Man: I'll bet.

Woman: Anyway, when I got to my feet and looked over the fence, Fred was quietly perched on Betty's shoulder – (he) was looking at me as if I was a complete moron.

Unit 5 Changes

Exercise 4a

Listen to the conversation and answer the questions in your book.

Man: . . . so I've started doing stretching exercises and press-ups and sit-ups before I go to work in the morning and I run up the stairs whenever I get the chance.

Woman: Why don't you try running or swimming or something like that to exercise your heart and lungs?

Man: Well I don't like jogging. I've tried it a few times but – well, frankly I find it boring, and there's nowhere to swim around here.

Woman: Yes there is. What about the Harold Hope Centre?

Man: Oh sure, yes. The last time I went there the pool was full of leaves and I nearly froze to death.

Woman: Oh that must have been a few years ago, it's all changed now. The pool's got a roof for a start.

Man: What! You mean they've actually spent money on the place?

Woman: Yeah, quite a lot over the last two or three years – you wouldn't recognize it. They've added a big cafeteria at the back of the building which overlooks the pool, it's really

quite comfortable. You do your exercises, you have a shower and maybe a sauna, and then you go and relax over a cup of coffee.

Man: A sauna!

Woman: Yeah, the area where they had the old cafe has been completely redesigned. It's got a sauna and – I don't use them myself – but they've got sunbeds, too.

Man: God, it has changed. Are the showers any better than they used to be?

Woman: Oh they've got rid of the old baths they had in there – I think there was some kind of public health problem there. Anyway, they've smartened up the showers and there are loads of them now. The water's always hot, too, which wasn't true before.

Man: Don't remind me.

Woman: Actually they've swapped the men's and the women's changing rooms because there are a lot more women going than there used to be and there's more room in there for the women – so they tell me. You should come along. You know the gym they had?

Man: Yeah.

Woman: Well, they ripped everything out of there and it's now full of all those multi-gym machines and erm (Man: Oh yeah) . . . they've got this . . . kind of . . . you know those exercise bikes . . . well, they've got those and they've got those weight things where you pull them and all that stuff . . . and there's . . . you know . . . you just exercise all your muscles and hang upside down and . . .

Man: If that's what you want to do.

Woman: Yeah, if you wanna do it. But it's unrecognizable now.

Man: I pass the place quite often but I hadn't noticed anything different.

Woman: Oh well, that's because they haven't done much to the front of the building.

147

Man: Oh I see.

Woman: They've kind of changed the entrance a bit but nothing you'd really notice. The entrance hall where you go in, it's it's almost the same. They've just moved the reception desk to the other side, but it's like it was really.

Man: It might be worth a look. The trouble is you have to be a member, don't you? Doesn't that cost quite a lot?

Woman: No, they've changed it so you can go in just for the day, or the evening or whatever and you pay a fixed fee. It's not members only any more. In fact, if you go regularly, it's certainly worth taking out membership, it's more economical in the long run.

Man: I'm definitely interested. It's open in the evenings, you say?

Woman: Yeah, actually, I'm going tomorrow – if you fancy a guided tour you can come with me.

Man: Oh yeah, yeah that'd be nice. Yes, it's a bit embarrassing if you're standing there in your trendy shorts without . . .

Unit 6   Revision and expansion

Exercise 5b

Listen and check your answers.

1 bruise   cruise   ruin   suit   fruit
2 leather   heal   sweat   healthy   spread
3 author   thorough   ruthless   thin   bother
4 hay   pale   vary   vague   phrase
5 honest   hour   huge   knee   knowledge

Exercise 10b

Listen and check your answers.

reliable   symptoms   hepatitis
pint   shy   prejudice   wrist
dynamic   cynic   tiny   agile
promise   wipe out   symphony

Unit 8   Prepositions and phrases

Exercise 1a

Listen and follow the instructions in your book.

Iris: You've got to tell me something that you're fond of. Right Joan.
Joan: Anything that I'm fond of.
Iris: Yeah.
Joan: Uh, swimming.
Iris: Mm. How about you Nick?
Nick: I'm fond of my two cats.
Iris: Aah. OK. Interests. Something that you're interested in. Anything.
Nick: I like to play with a brass band.
Iris: That's your interest.
Nick: If I get a chance.
Joan: I'm interested in fell walking.
Iris: Oh, you've got to say something you're afraid of.
Joan: Snakes, undoubtedly . . . snakes.
Nick: Oh, um . . .
Iris: Phobias?
Nick: Phobias. Oh death, I suppose. The big one.
Iris: Worried about?
Nick: Oh, where's wheres's my next job coming from, I think.
Joan: Yeah, likewise. And being late.
Iris: Being late.
Nick: Yeah.
Iris: Jobs. Right. Ah, this is good. What are you good at?
Joan: Swimming.
Iris: Jolly good.
Nick: Mmm, yes . . .
Iris: Come on.
Nick: I can't think of anything I'm good at . . . I'm good at playing my brass instrument.
Iris: Oh, that's your interest. And oh, and what are you shocked by?

Nick: Tabloid newspapers.

Joan: Exactly the same. I was just gonna say that . . . and, shocked by . . . when I put on the radio and hear Tony Blackburn on Capital Gold coming out with things you read in tabloid newspapers.

(Yes, yes)

Iris: Allergic to?

Joan: Strawberries.

Nick: Mmm . . . (Tabloid newspapers?) A pen . . . a penicillin called Vibramycin. It makes me sick.

Iris: Oh, now what are you looking forward to?

Joan: Going away at Christmas.

Nick: Going away just after Christmas – to Africa.

Iris: Oh. Now, what are you thinking of doing fairly soon? Eating?

Joan: Meeting a friend at lunch time.

Nick: I'm going to visit my sister in Reading.

Unit 10   Affixation

Exercise 2c

Listen to the five passages and follow the instructions in your book.

1 Well, he didn't get to work till . . . till gone ten – by which time I was already pretty angry, and when he walked through the door I . . . I just lost my temper and we had this dreadful row.

2 The wedding reception would've been lovely except that Mathew made a complete nuisance of himself all afternoon and even started taking the paper off some of the wedding presents.

3 Originally we . . . we thought he was exactly the right person for the job – steady, reliable, conscientious you know. But he's just thrown money away on ridiculous schemes and we

could find ourselves in serious financial trouble at this rate.

4 The committe definitely gave us the impression they were going to consult the members on the question of a new treasurer before taking any action. Now we discover they've already had a meeting and voted in that fool Hopkins for another two years.

5 It was awful. I'd already spent half an hour with one doctor and then another one came along and told me to take my clothes off because they weren't entirely happy and wanted to have another look at my back.

Unit 12   Revision and expansion

Exercise 5b

Listen and check your answers.

voyage	channel	canal
dessert	desert	commute
average	cottage	antique
resort	hotel	hazard
addict	collide	recruit

Unit 14   Verbs

Exercise 3c

Listen to the story of Carmen and follow the instructions in your book.

Woman: I wouldn't mind seeing Carmen . . . I don't really know what it's about, though.

Man: Oh, it's quite an exciting story . . . umm about a gypsy woman called Carmen, and it takes place around a cigar factory in . . . uh Seville, I think it is. And the other main character is a soldier, Don Jose. And the two of them meet for the first time when Carmen – arriving in town – gets into a fight with another woman, and . . .

Woman: It's not very ladylike.

Man: No, she's a pretty tough piece of work. Anyway, Don Jose arrests her and puts her in prison, but she manages to escape because he falls asleep while guarding her – then gets put in prison himself for being so incompetent.

Woman: Sounds pretty unlikely, doesn't it?

Man: Well, it is opera, remember. Anyway, uh . . . later on, they meet again in a bar and Carmen starts teasing him and making fun of him. By this point though, Don Jose has fallen in love with her.

Woman: Naturally.

Man: Oh yeah. I mean, she's a very kind of powerful seductive woman.

Woman: Sort of *femme fatale*?

Man: Yeah exactly. And uh . . . when he sees Carmen surrounded by other men, Don Jose gets madly jealous and picks a fight with one of them, a bullfighter. Anyway, it all builds up to this climax at the end.

Woman: What happens in the fight?

Man: Oh, not a lot, not a lot. The bullfighter eventually leaves but Don Jose prevents Carmen from going off with him. Anyway, at the end of the story, as I was saying, at the end, there's a big bullfight, featuring, of course, this bullfighter. But when Don Jose sees Carmen at the entrance, he refuses to let her in. And that's followed by a big argument and in the end Carmen pulls out a knife and stabs him. But then, full of remorse, she gives herself up.

Woman: And that's it?

Man: Yeah.

Woman: It's real soap opera stuff, isn't it?

Man: Yeah well, I mean, if you want to see something else . . .

Unit 15   Choices

Exercise 3b

Listen to the conversation and follow the instructions in your book.

Man: . . . but it's really quite handy because I can get the bus just down the road, which takes me to Shepherds Bush. Then, I get another bus and that drops me right outside the office.

Woman: Oh, and how long does it take?

Man: Well, if I'm lucky, about half an hour . . . but it really depends on the traffic and how long I have to hang around waiting for a bus. They're supposed to run every five minutes, but if you believe that, you'll believe anything. And, uh, on a bad day the journey can take anything up to an hour.

Woman: Well, surely the underground must be quicker than that?

Man: Actually not that much, no, because I've got to walk to Ealing Broadway to get the tube, and that's about ten minutes, then there's another five to ten minutes walk when I get off at Holland Park. It takes about half an hour, but it's more expensive than the bus, of course.

Woman: Well, how much more?

Man: Well, if you get a monthly travel card, it works out at about a pound a day.

Woman: And how much does the bus cost?

Man: About 70p; it's quite a difference.

Woman: Yeah. Why don't you take the car?

Man: Well, I used to drive in quite a lot; it's handy if the weather's bad and if you've got something to do – shopping and that – on the way home. But recently, the traffic's been getting really bad – if you get stuck in Shepherds Bush, it can take forty-five minutes to drive, what, five miles. It's just not worth the hassle unless you're travelling out of the rushhour, and recently I've started cycling in. (Oh.) I can take a short cut through the park.

Woman: Acton Park?

Man: Yeah. You're not actually meant to cycle in the park and if they catch you it's a twenty-five pound fine. But loads of people do ride so . . . I doubt if they'd actually prosecute anyone, and . . .

Woman: But hang on, you've still got to come through Shepherds Bush, haven't you? That must be really dangerous on a bike.

Man: Yeah, it can be a bit scary. Most drivers don't take any notice of cyclists so you've got to have your wits about you. But I quite enjoy the challenge. Mind you, I'm not sure how keen I'll be on cycling once the weather gets bad. At the moment though, it's definitely the quickest way to get to work.

Woman: And the cheapest.

Man: Yeah and the cheapest, although if you buy all the right gear for cycling it works out quite expensive. This crash helmet cost me a fortune and these . . .

Unit 17 Technology

Exercise 3b

Listen to the six short conversations and complete the chart in your book.

1 A: I started getting interference about a month ago but it's got much worse.
  B: Since when?
  A: The last few days. It keeps flickering and I can't get a proper picture at all for more than about five minutes.

2 A: I was happily working away and suddenly the thing just packed up.
  B: Mm. Could be a faulty connection.

A: No, I don't think so. I checked the plug and the lead – they're OK.
  B: Well, perhaps some dust or dirt has got into it.
  A: Maybe, but I've only made a couple of small holes in the wall, and it was fine the last time I used it.

3 A: I can't understand it. It's going right the way through the cycle and seems to be working OK, but when I take the things out they're still damp.
  B: Well, they're meant to be, aren't they?
  A: No, not that much. There's definitely something wrong with it, and it's leaking a bit. Look, can you see that water mark on the floor?
  B: Oh yeah. You'd better call a plumber in that case.

4 A: What's the matter?
  B: I can't get this thing to wind on. It's supposed to be automatic when you take a picture.
  A: Is the battery OK?
  B: I dunno. Well, it should be.

5 A: D'you know anything about these things?
  B: No, not a lot. What's the problem?
  A: I think the paper's getting jammed. They're not coming through.
  B: Mmm. There's a bit of a burning smell, as well. Let's take a look inside.
  A: How d'you open it?
  B: There's a lever at the side; just push it down and it releases the top.

6 A: Oh this damn thing.
  B: What's the matter now?
  A: Oh these keys keep sticking.
  B: Well, I'm not surprised – it's about thirty years old. Why don't you buy an electronic one?
  A: Cos I'm saving up for a computer, that's why.

Unit 17, Exercise 4a

Listen to the different noises and follow the numbers in your book.

The eight sounds on the tape are all described in the Student Book on page 75.

Unit 18   Revision and expansion

Exercise 5b

Listen and check your answers.

ambulance	psychology	
necessary	instrument	corruption
emergency	interested	
thermometer	presumably	
microphone	document	
potentially	paragraph	
alternative	temperature	
machinery		

Unit 19   Customs

Exercise 1b

Listen to the conversation and follow the instructions in your book.

Woman: So shaking hands in England. David, what do you think?

David: Erm . . . formal formal introduction – yes.

Woman: Yes. Mandy?

Mandy: Yes I'd go along with that.

Woman: I would, it's usual. The next one. What about shaking hands with colleagues?

David: Er no.

Mandy: No.

David: That is very continental isn't it? (Yes) Not British at all.

Woman: Not at all. No.

David: It would take too much time.

Woman: Absolutely. What about English people shaking hands with children? I don't think I've ever seen English people shaking hands.

David: Only doing a sort of of 'I'm treating you as a grown-up' type of man to man thing but not really.

Woman: But it is not a regular thing, is it, it is not a form of greeting.

Mandy: It is as an adult man to a younger adult, (Yeah, yeah) a teenager or something.

David: Yes, I'll treat you as an equal (Yes, you're a man now) but otherwise not.

Woman: But not with children?

David: No.

Woman: And English people kissing friends as a form of greeting?

Mandy: I think they do now.

Woman: I think so.

David: I think they do, certainly relatives and . . .

Woman: Yes, always within families usually, I think we could say.

David: Yes, I think I think people who know each other very well (So friends) people who come round to dinner or whatever.

Woman: Yes, then you'd kiss friends as a form of greeting.

Mandy: So this is wrong, isn't it.

David: But that's kind of new.

Woman: Yes it is new, but I think that is false because we do it. What about addressing somebody as 'Sir' or 'Madam' if you didn't know their name?

Mandy: Oh dear. I wouldn't do it now.

David: No, I think because the class thing has kind of evaporated to some extent I don't regard anybody as 'Sir' or 'Madam' (No) in that sense – do you?

Woman: No. No no I tend to . . .

David: I think if one goes into shops but er shops or restaurants, but I mean (possibly) that's in a different somebody is in a different position then.

Woman: Absolutely, because somebody is serving somebody else.

David: That's right.

Woman: Not on a normal level, no, because one tends to assume equality . . . so wouldn't normally address them in that way. No. What about saying surnames first if you answer the telephone?

Mandy: Well I don't, definitely.

Woman: I don't either, no. Do you?

David: No I don't think I do.

Woman: Don't you say, 'hello'.

David: 'Hello' and well the number – I usually give the number.

Mandy: Oh, you give the number.

Woman: Have you heard anybody say their surname though if you you've phoned somebody?

David: No – not at all.

Mandy: No, I don't think I have.

Woman: So . . . that's totally false. What about asking people how much they earn?

David: Well I'll tell you if you like, (I don't want to know) but I think it is rude.

Mandy: I do want to know. We all want to know, but it is rude to ask.

Woman: It is rude – yes, financial matters are still quite difficult.

David: And I've known people who have tried to kind of break that barrier down – but it doesn't break down. (It doesn't, doesn't work) Not even among people who would have an . . . there would be an advantage by discussing, for instance ourselves, how much they're earning.

Woman: Quite, so it is it is a taboo thing isn't it?

David: I think it is, yes.

Woman: Yes, yes, Next one.

David: Number eight.

Woman: What about blowing one's nose in public? Bad manners, jolly bad.

David: Is it?

Mandy: I think it depends if you've got a handkerchief there inbetween.

David: If you give a really good old hoot, I think that is probably bad but I think it's . . .

Mandy: Yes, I think you're right . . .

Woman: But people wipe their noses in public, I mean, because its considered bad manners to sniff. Surely?

David: Or to drip.

Mandy: Quite.

Woman: Quite, so it's politer to blow your nose.

David: Well I think so.

Woman: Absolutely, it's more polite.

Mandy: But it is still a bit like sneezing. You say 'Oh sorry'.

David: Yes, you you probably would say . . . actually I think it's you would say 'sorry' after sneezing.

Mandy: . . . it depend on your proximity?

David: Yes it does.

Mandy: If we're very close and I blow my nose that's not very nice. (No) If I did it discreetly –

Woman: But it is better than sniffing. (Yes. Yes.)

David: I wouldn't agree with that.

Woman: No but it is quite hard to generalize, because is it bad manners to blow one's nose at the table?

Mandy: Yes, I think it is.

Woman: But it is also bad manners to sniff . . . to sniff at the table (you can't win) – so it is quite difficult to reach a conclusion.

David: Yes, it is difficult.

Woman: What about: people saying 'good morning' or 'good afternoon' to a shop assistant when they are served?

David: Well I try to. It depends erm sometimes you get this terrible kind of Gorgon-like stare from the shop assistant and nobody says anything.

Mandy: But is it as a goodbye or hello?

David: It depends. It tends to depend on the shop.

Woman: When you are being served, I mean; would you walk in and would you say 'good morning'?

Mandy: No.

Woman: Oh.

David: No. I think if it was a small shop, but I mean obviously in a supermarket when you come up to the check-out you don't particularly say good morning.

Woman: No quite, because it is more impersonal, but if you went into a small shop . . .?

Mandy: Yes you might do.

David: You might.

Mandy: . . . and also to get their attention.

Woman: Yes and I actually try to, just to . . . to be polite and create a sort of ambience.

David: Yes and I resent it if it is not returned.

Woman: Quite – so it is difficult to generalize there because of the size of the shop, but a small shop you would.

David: I think so, yes.

Woman: What about the last question, number ten. In a restaurant, attracting a waiter's attention?

David: Never – I don't think I have ever said 'Waiter'. I (I have never) know people who do though.

Woman: Yes I have heard it, but doesn't it jar?

Mandy: Yes.

Woman: Yes. So you'd never call out 'Waiter'.

David: No – it's 'excuse me'. I don't know whether I address them as anything really.

Woman: I usually just try to to (wave) or eye contact.

(Yes, yes)

David: 'Excuse me' – 'May I'?

Woman: Mmm. But never call out 'Waiter'.

(No)

David: Although it should be said that some people do.

Woman: Yes, absolutely.

Unit 21   Men and women

Exercise 2b

Listen and follow the instructions in your book.

A: No, he doesn't object at all.

B: Well, if a job has to be done, I realize that I'll have to sacrifice some of my free time.

C: Yes I think so. I'm used to working under pressure and I think I handle it quite well.

D: Yes, one of each.

E: Well, even if I knew the answer to that I'm not sure I'd be willing to let you in on the secret.

F: Oh, I'm rather looking forward to that actually.

G: No I doubt that very much; we're pretty settled where we are.

H: Well, I think that would depend on how serious it was.

I: Well, it's very difficult to make a promise like that at this stage, but I certainly don't look upon this position as a temporary one.

J: We've got a child minder.

K: I can't really say . . . I'd have to discuss it with my husband and, of course, much would depend on what I was being promoted to.

L: She's an accountant.

Unit 22   Ways of saying things

Exercise 2b

Listen to the sentences and follow the instructions in your book.

1   There's no hurry – we've got loads of time.

2   When will dinner be ready? I'm starving.

3   The flat's next to the underground, which is very handy for work.

4 The kids will be going back to school next week.

5 Word processing may seem difficult at first, but once you get the hang of it, it's easy.

6 Hey, someone's pinched my dictionary.

7 The others liked the film but I though it was a real drag.

8 I bet you'll be pleased when the conference is over.

9 What's up?

10 We really need a company with know-how for this contract.

11 It's not an easy exam but I reckon she'll pass.

12 D'you fancy a bite to eat before we go out?

Unit 24   Revision and expansion

Exercise 5b

Listen and check your answers.

rude	flood	stood	mood
bully	hug	shove	prove
butcher	customary		enthusiastic
root	cushion	dull	cucumber
luxury			

Unit 24, Exercise 9b

Listen and check your answers.

suit	yacht	chaos	quite
quiet	react	ruin	reach
naked	shocked	poem	bias
doubt	riot	fares	whereas
suede	client	fuel	queue